Activism and Social Change

# ACTIVISM
## and
## SOCIAL CHANGE

*LESSONS for* **COMMUNITY ORGANIZING** *2nd edition*

Eric Shragge

UNIVERSITY OF TORONTO PRESS

Library and Archives Canada Cataloguing in Publication

Shragge, Eric, 1948–
  Activism and social change : lessons for community organizing / Eric Shragge. — 2nd ed.

Includes bibliographical references and index. Issued also in electronic format.
ISBN 978-1-4426-0627-2 (pbk.).—ISBN 978-1-4426-0770-5 (bound)

  1. Community organization.  2. Social action.  I. Title.

HM831.S53 2013                   361.8                 C2012-908021-7

We welcome comments and suggestions regarding any aspect of our publications— please feel free to contact us at news@utphighereducation.com or visit our Internet site at www.utppublishing.com.

*North America*
5201 Dufferin Street
North York, Ontario, Canada, M3H 5T8

2250 Military Road
Tonawanda, New York, USA, 14150

ORDERS PHONE: 1–800–565–9523
ORDERS FAX: 1–800–221–9985
ORDERS E-MAIL: utpbooks@utpress.utoronto.ca

*UK, Ireland, and continental Europe*
NBN International
Estover Road, Plymouth, PL6 7PY, UK
ORDERS PHONE: 44 (0) 1752 202301
ORDERS FAX: 44 (0) 1752 202333
ORDERS E-MAIL:
enquiries@nbninternational.com

Every effort has been made to contact copyright holders; in the event of an error or omission, please notify the publisher.

This book is printed on paper containing 100% post-consumer fibre.

The University of Toronto Press acknowledges the financial support for its publishing activities of the Government of Canada through the Canada Book Fund.

Printed in Canada

RECYCLED
Paper made from
recycled material
FSC® C103567

# CONTENTS

# INTRODUCTION TO THE SECOND EDITION

I am writing the introduction to the second edition of this book in September 2012. The last couple of years have been remarkable. Popular uprisings have challenged power across the globe, toppling long-standing regimes in Tunisia and Egypt. In Europe, government-imposed austerity has been met with occupations and street battles. The Occupy movement sprang up across North America last fall and winter. Closer to home in Quebec, the battle against tuition fee increases became the vehicle to challenge the neo-liberal direction of successive governments. More important were the massive demonstrations, estimated between 200,000 and 300,000 people, and the ability of students to shut down educational institutions for months and rally allies from unions, community organizations, and social movements. Street battles, mass arrests, and brutal police repression were nightly occurrences, culminating in legislation designed to limit the right to demonstrate, suspending the school term in striking universities and colleges, and forcing students back for an extra term in August. The legislation was defied by a demonstration of more than 200,000, and the student leaders deliberately broke the law by not providing their route. Some have said this was the largest act of collective civil disobedience in Canadian history. In neighbourhoods across the province, a "casserole" movement took to the streets, banging pots and pans and defying the law. In my neighbourhood one evening, more than 200 people created a huge racket as they marched to the front of the Premier Jean Charest's home, while the police directed traffic. Popular assemblies have been organized to direct further protest activities. The government called an election and after a short campaign found itself in opposition with its leader losing his seat. The new minority government has delivered on its promise to freeze tuition and repeal the repressive legislation. The victory is a tribute to the power of mass movements, defiance of repression, and a capacity to mobilize a base. We celebrate this victory! In many ways the massive protests, local mobilization, and polarization became a proxy for the wider questions about the economic and social direction of Quebec. Large popular mobilizations like this are exceptions and do not last for long periods, but their impact is much longer if victories are won. The student movement is the only group in Quebec that has successfully fought governments' attempts to impose or raise user fees (tuition) as part of the larger policy agenda of service cuts and privatization. Will this movement be able to continue or will it dissipate as people return to their daily lives, jobs, and families while students are in classes making up for the long strike?

At a more personal level, in the School of Community and Public Affairs, where I taught for the past twelve years, students struck at both at the graduate and undergraduate levels, and there were virtually no classes for the last seven weeks of term. The graduate students, along with others, organized a demonstration in front of the condo of the acting university president, exposing his subsidized mortgage in a time when the university supported tuition increases as a response to inadequate government funding of higher education. It was my last term of teaching before my retirement. I did not want to leave without some kind of final student encounter; I organized an informal discussion open to anyone, which I called "What I learned from the strike." To begin the discussion, I talked about my experience in the Black Action Movement university strike when I was a student (see below) and the importance it had for me. Many issues were raised, including the importance of being part of the strike movement as a learning experience, the frustrations of mobilizing others, and the fears of personal "burnout." There was a mix of pride, optimism about the power of collective action, and stress because of the sleepless nights and the intensity of this period of organizing. The lessons that the students learned are the universal ones—in particular, how mass mobilization and collective action can challenge power. The experience we shared was a moment in the history of the popular movement in Quebec. Perhaps more important in the long term is the impact of the strike, and of the many demonstrations, confrontations with authorities, and other actions in the process of political learning. Two elements interact here—the first lesson is the understanding of power, how it operates, and in whose interests it works. Second, there is a question of who shares this interest and who will support and defend those with power. The student strike polarized Quebec society. The specific demands for a tuition freeze quickly became symbolic for the direction of the social and economic development of the society—in other words, neo-liberalism. Those opposed to this direction included the unions, the community sector, and the range of social movement organizations. The biggest difference was the large number of people who were not part of the "usual suspects," yet took to the streets in demonstrations to support the students and oppose the repressive government legislation and ongoing police violence. Throughout the period, it became clear who was on what side—big business and the mainstream media all seemed to deplore the strike and related action while a large number of "red squares"—the symbol of the strike—became visible across the city. A related lesson is that all of the protests and confrontations make power relations clear and can force shifts in policy. At the end, it became clear that the Charest government could only move ahead with a new mandate, as his administration had lost credibility with so many across the province. Faced with mass demonstrations and disruptions in the downtown core of Montreal, the government's recourse was either to increase repression, which had not been effective in quelling the unrest, or to show it had broad support through an election. Neither one worked.

A lasting lesson is that sustained action, mass mobilization, smart leadership, and building good relations with allies can force change. Underlying this victory is a lesson about building and sustaining a base, one that can be mobilized, and showing support for the campaign. The movement of students was decentralized. Strike mandates came from local associations through departmental assemblies, which debated the issues and made decisions about whether or not to participate in the strike. Without the local organization in colleges and universities across the province, the day-to-day activities required to keep institutions and departments closed would not have happened and the mass mobilizations would not have had a base. It is clear that there is no shortcut; local work is essential. It is at this level that education and argumentation on the issues is best, that leadership emerges, and that mobilization happens. The success of the student movement happened at least in a large part because of local organizing. In the movement's most intense period, emotional and personal support, and finding the collective courage to enter into difficult confrontations, occurred through local networks. There is a key lesson here that connects with the book that follows. Without local organizing, agitating, educating, and leadership-building, broader change is impossible—*but*, without "the movement," bigger campaigns, alliances, and coalition-building, local organizations cannot contribute to wider social change and can fall into insular activity, whether that is service provision or attempting very limited campaigns on very limited issues. The challenges are there and the goal of this book is to analyze and examine local work through the lens of community organizing.

# INTRODUCTION: ASKING HARD QUESTIONS

## INTRODUCTION

Community organizing has been a central part of my life for more than forty years. On some days, I feel that I have reached an understanding of what it is and what can be accomplished through it; on others, the uncertainties are nagging. I have been involved in many different roles, campaigns, projects, and organizations. It would be easy to idealize these experiences and to argue that community organizing has made an important contribution to changing the fabric of North American society, but I am not a simple promoter. I have moved between periods of optimism and profound pessimism about the role of the community movement and what it has and can accomplish. "Accomplish" implies a normative stance. What do I mean by that? Perhaps this is the central question for this book. How does one judge what community organizing should be trying to do? Here the question of where one stands is crucial, since that dictates the types of questions and definitions one uses and what values and political traditions shape those questions and form one's standpoint. This chapter acts as a launching pad for a reflection and a critical discussion of community organizing. The book itself looks back and forward. It tries to capture the traditions and meanings of organizing practice, starting from my experiences and widening the lens. In this chapter, I will discuss my own development and experiences of practice. I have chosen to use autobiographical elements in this chapter in order to raise the questions and issues that shape the rest of the book. My own experiences reflect wider practices and focus on the years between the late 1960s and now. The examples that I draw upon will illustrate some of the diversity of these issues and related practices and will be a means of entering into the debates and lessons.

Although I spent thirty-nine years teaching in a university setting, I hope this book will depart from academic traditions. It begins with politics and practice, but draws on some useful academic sources. It will always come back to the politics of practice, referring to the key question on the role of community organizing in promoting and participating in the processes of progressive social change. I will avoid specific and narrow definitions of these terms for the moment. In general, I am drawing on the belief that the process that leads to social change begins when large numbers of people act in their own self-interest, and act collectively to promote economic and social justice. In the process of working for these ideals, it is necessary and indeed equally important to expand democratic opportunities and increase the control of people over the institutions that affect their lives. In other words, there are political and social ends that are defined by material gains and changing relations of power. Perhaps this is too idealistic a position for our pragmatic world of partnership and deal-making, but it is the starting point for me, and will act as a crude benchmark for later discussions.

Why did I decide to write the first edition of this book? There is an easy answer and more complex answer. The easy one is that I began this project on sabbatical leave from my job. Writing this book seemed like a good project to undertake during that period. The real and deeper answer is that I felt out of step with many of the practices and the beliefs found in community organizations when I began writing. This feeling was not recent; it had been building for many years. In many ways, my orientation is from an earlier period, shaped by the ideals of the 1960s and the political and social analyses and perspectives that grew out of that period, and so I subsequently learned more about the traditions of the "Left." I have witnessed the changes in the community movement since then. There are positive developments, but at the same time, there has been a loss of the movement's critical edge and engagement in the wider struggle for economic and social justice. With the deterioration of social and economic conditions for many, community organizations have become part of the system—part of the problem, rather than a source of opposition to the forces that have reshaped the economy and social life. The book examines the changes, the forces that have led to its redefinition, and seeks a way to learn lessons from the past, critique the present, and find new paths on which to move forward.

I begin my discussion with some basic questions. Why community organizing, how did I get into it, what were the processes, and what has changed in practice over the years? For the sake of clarity, I will overstate my position and then nuance it later. Community organizing at its best creates sites and practices of opposition. Those interested in progressive social change, social justice, and so on were attracted to the community movement because it was a place to organize resistance to the system of global capitalism, patriarchy, racism, and other forms of socio-economic oppression and domination. They believed that the local community—the neighbourhood—was a place where people could meet to challenge those forces that oppressed them and, in the process, learn about the relationships between personal issues and the wider forces that shape them. Forms of collective action are the products of the meeting of the personal and the political. Clearly there is a lot more to all of this, but this is what is at the core of community organization. People may be interested in community for a variety of other reasons but for me the reason for participation in local activities is the potential to build strong opposition. I am not only talking about protest and confrontation, but the creation of democratic opportunities in which people can learn about their collective strengths and build social solidarity. In the community, there can be a variety of practices that may not seem oppositional but within them there are practices that question relations of power, build alternative visions, and shift power to those who usually do not have it. In other words, working in the community sector is a political opportunity—and one that can be taken and used to promote social change.

The second part of the response to the question of why I am involved with community organizing is more personal. I came from a secure, middle-class home with professional parents who valued success in their children in traditional terms. How did I end up caring about these issues and over such a long period of time? It is no longer trendy to consider oneself as unambiguously on the left—the untraditional, libertarian left influenced by both Marxists and anarchists. There are not many out there with me and my viewpoint does not often find itself expressed in the corporate-dominated media. More to the point, I rarely see these perspectives and beliefs among those involved in most community organizations. Frankly, I'm often unsure of where people stand, perhaps as vague social democrats or as progressive pragmatics trying to make life a little more tolerable for those on the margins. How did I end up here? Many people from similar backgrounds were radical in their youth but there are few that have maintained their engagement over many years.

Where did the trip start? Perhaps it was exposure to a tradition of social justice through synagogue affiliation and related youth movements? I have clear memories of a presentation of a young man who went to participate in civil rights struggles in the early 1960s in the southern USA, and his discussion of the promotion of non-violence and the violence he experienced in return. I remember trying to convince a Hebrew school-teacher that, based on principles of justice in the Jewish traditions, being a communist was a more appropriate ideology than supporting capitalism. But I had little exposure in my home to the old left of the previous generation, except through a couple of friends of my parents. On the other hand, my parents reminded my brothers and me of our privilege relative to most others. My grandparents were immigrants and poverty was only a generation removed from us. Another factor perhaps was not fitting in well or feeling comfortable with the in crowd. By high school I was more intellectually intense and serious than most of my peers. It must have been something there that sparked my interest in the events of the 1960s, and encouraged me to see that there was something profound happening. By my third year at university (1968) the world was coming undone and my consciousness was forming. I quickly learned who was on which side, and I had begun to understand that there are no givens without challenge. I participated in a few protests at that time, and I began to learn that the radical challenge of the period had profound roots and ideas that were often lost as a result of the period's style.

I fell into organizing partly by accident and partly as a product of the time. I did an undergraduate degree at McGill University between 1965 and 1969. I lived through a period when universities exploded with student activism: I was only peripherally involved in that period but was part of a group of Jewish students that challenged the priorities of that community and got a hearing by threatening to disrupt a Passover service at a rich Westmount synagogue. I was also in a group in the Genetics Department that demanded student representation on departmental committees. But, looking back, I think that for me the images of the period were probably greater than the social understanding and knowledge I gained. I remember a picture of a male student with long, dishevelled hair and a beard seated in a university board of governors member's chair during an occupation. I remember the snowballs thrown by engineering students at a large group (of which I was one) protesting the firing of a left-wing activist political science teacher. By the late 1960s, the campus was theatre. People were organizing both on and off it. The key campaign was against the United States' war against the people in Vietnam. On campus, we demanded an extension of democracy with parity of students on university committees and decision-making bodies. We argued that universities had to be part of a critical reflection on the injustices in society, and therefore be part of the opposition to corporate capitalism.

I felt pulled by the excitement of the period, the sense of optimism that social change and justice were possible. We believed as a generation that we would make a major contribution to that process. During that time, I was involved in the Jewish community, and I worked at a synagogue and the YM-YWHA as a youth worker as well with teens at a summer camp. By 1968, I had decided that I wanted a career in social work. It wasn't a difficult decision; my grades in my genetics courses were only okay and I did not think that chasing fruit flies around a laboratory or doing genetic counselling would keep me interested for very long. Besides, the world was changing out there and I wanted to be a part of it. I knew very little about social work but I thought that it would allow me to make some positive social contributions. So off I went to the University of Michigan in Ann Arbor to become a social worker. I was naive, had a strong sense of right and wrong, and firm opinions about social justice, but I was a political illiterate. I had no sense of the traditions of the left that would play such an important part of my life. My education in the biological sciences at McGill left me with little in the way of tools for social analysis. But somehow the challenges to authority, the questioning of the legitimacy of the social order, got through and shaped my identity. I began to see myself as a radical, to use the jargon of the period. I don't think I knew what that meant, except that it was a visceral antagonism to the major social and economic institutions. If asked at the time, I don't think that I would have placed myself on the left. To me that meant either social democrats and/or pro–Soviet Union communists. Neither had any appeal—they still don't, but more on that later!

My political formation and definition as an activist really began in the School of Social Work at the University of Michigan. I entered immediately after my undergraduate degree, leaving to live away from home long-term for the first time. My previous experiences did not prepare me for the two years that followed. My first field placement was in an inner-city school; as well, I volunteered with both the tenants' union to support a large successful rent strike and with a centre for street kids; and during the summer, with a few others, I participated in a recruiting drive for a welfare rights organization. I met people who legitimated, for me, both the necessity for radical social change and my desire to be part of it. It was not always easy. I felt intimidated by more experienced and knowledgeable activists. But it got better as I began to find a place. I became more confident about my own identity as a radical, someone who was trying to find a way to live a life that incorporated social change activities as a central component. I wanted to pursue a career as a community organizer and I decided that mainstream social work was not for me. I was fortunate because it was a period in which community organizing had legitimacy in the profession.

As part of this reflection I want to recall images of that period that convey its spirit. This will not be a process of glorification of the past, but rather an attempt to describe my experiences. My memory has become selective over time, but, keeping in mind that the goal of this exercise is to understand the present, these lessons, images, and ideas will all help. Some of these images remain with me today as powerful reminders of those early experiences. I remember some of the welfare recipients, their strength to not only survive but to challenge the oppression of poverty in the USA. I remember one woman in particular with scars from suicide attempts on her wrists; she was a leader who, along with her Black friend, held sit-ins in the churches of Ann Arbor demanding reparations for the church's support of slavery. Courage was necessary. The year before I had arrived for graduate school, the local sheriff had called out the dogs to attack a peaceful demonstration of welfare mothers. There was a risk involved, but this was how we understood what we referred to then as "Amerika." I remember one story from my field placement in an inner-city school in Detroit. A Black youngster eight or ten years old told me about hiding under his bed while tanks drove down his street. The polarization in the society was real—White kids busted for drugs, the Black Panthers facing the police who had declared war on them, some young men going to jail or fleeing to avoid the draft, and an anti-authoritarian youth culture that did not know its left from its right. One of the first and most important lessons I learned was that I was an outsider, despite what I believed and the solidarity I could offer. I was not poor, I was White, privileged, educated, and I had many potential life choices. As I became more active over the years that followed, I learned that trust was something that had to be earned. It came with time, respect, and a willingness to listen and to act in support and not to take over. At the same time, there should always be a tension in the relationship. We may bring skills, knowledge, and a useful status to a group or a struggle, but at the same time we have to know our place; the reason we are there is to help build a democratic option where people can have control and a voice. This was an early and key lesson for me.

Other images of the time: the Black Action Movement strike that shut down the university for more than a week demanding increased Black admissions and support. I remember getting up at five in the morning to picket at the university heating plant because the union had said that if there were a picket line it would not cross it. Heavy, wet snow, rain, and slush over our shoes did not deter us. It was an important lesson for me—understanding the necessity of links between organized labour and social movements. Also, I learned about the power of numbers to disrupt and shut institutions and to win concessions because of the process. The times were exciting. For me, it was the beginning of a political process believing that opposition to the established powers and values was necessary. The solidarity between people was growing and the playing out of social conflict was at a high. These were not experiences that were unique and I was in no way central to the process. I remained on the margins, did my bit, and learned profound lessons. But it was the beginning. I knew that there was something in community organizing that could link my emerging political orientation with a way to express it. Those were the times when all seemed possible. With the right combination of commitment and moral fibre, we could accomplish anything.

Over the years that followed, I have found many ways to stay involved. I will describe a few of these and examine some of the questions that they raised and the lessons that I learned from them. I have chosen the following for discussion: neighbourhood organizing, peace movement activities, and a return to the former. I will examine other practical experiences in the chapters that follow. Below, I will present a critical reflection—a type of examination that has shaped much of scholarship and one that grows from experiences in the field and an analysis of that practice.

## NEIGHBOURHOOD ORGANIZING

In 1974, I was hired by the School of Social Work at McGill University. My job was classified as a field instructor, mandated to develop field placements for students in the community and to supervise their work. The school had already developed a placement with a small recreation association in a working-class area. Residents were housed in three-floor walk-up apartment buildings hastily built after the Second World War which, although privately owned, were subsided through long-term, low-interest mortgages provided through a federal government housing program. I think the small group that ran the recreation association and those at the School of Social Work would have been happier if I had put in place a tutorial service and an after-school program for kids. I was, however, strongly influenced by Saul Alinsky, an American community organizer, as well as the New Left (more on these later), and I wanted to organize people to take on issues that affected their lives, such as housing and neighbourhood conditions. Besides, I had to supervise six students who were keen to try something different. So we embarked on a period of intense door-knocking, speaking to as many residents as we could. Students were paired and assigned to a street. The issues identified were typical: lack of repairs in apartments, unsafe conditions in the alleys, and so on. We brought small groups together, meeting in peoples' homes or in the recreation centre, which was a small basement apartment. We got people to move into action; we won some concessions and made a bit of a name for ourselves. The first landlord we took on was a prominent physician. In order to get him to negotiate, tenants picketed his house in an upper-class neighbourhood and walked into his clinic. These events were covered in the media, and they finally brought him to the negotiating table with his lawyer in tow. He agreed to the demands of the tenants but subsequently sold his property. These types of activities created tension with those in charge of the recreation centre, whose leaders felt they were connected to the government of the city and indirectly to the mayor at the time, Jean Drapeau. However, despite their opposition, there was enough support to create an independent neighbourhood organization that was called POWER (Peoples' Organization of Westhaven Elmhurst Residents).

.I was fortunate to be able to affiliate with Parallel Institute, an organizing centre in Pointe St. Charles, which was a working-class district with a tradition of activism. The organizing staff at Parallel had recently broadened their orientation from welfare rights to one based on neighbourhood organizing. For several years the work that my students and I did was linked to the work of that institute as it established organizations in other working-class communities. All of these organizing drives achieved concrete gains, improving housing, municipal services, and other conditions. In addition, organizers identified local leaders and trained them to play public and active roles in the development of the organizations. The structures were based on committees formed on city blocks and these were joined together to form the larger group. However, all of the organizers and some of the leaders recognized the limits of local work. A couple of campaigns were run based on common issues such as the city of Montreal's refusal to post and enforce twenty-mile-per–hour traffic zones, and the lack of beat police. These were relatively successful and a coalition of local organizations forced the city to make concessions. Disruptive tactics, such as the occupation of a city-owned restaurant, and confrontations with high-ranking officials were key actions in these campaigns. Their power came from the mobilization of large numbers of people. This was an important aspect of the work, a central principle, one that has been forgotten by many community workers and their organizations today.

Larger campaigns were envisioned, such as challenging the rate structures and other policies of the natural gas and hydroelectric companies. The idea behind these was to enlarge the base of the organizing and bring representatives from other groups to these actions. We were not successful in achieving these goals. There was suspicion among French-speaking popular organizations, who had developed a different style and priorities, as well as among other more conventional groups, who did not invest a lot of energy in these actions. The failure of these campaigns and our impatience with the limits of local work in getting at some of the basic class and broader social questions led to a gradual abandonment of these efforts. The group that I had organized went through other incarnations and continued for several years after my departure.

These experiences brought me many positive lessons and raised some questions. On the positive side, I learned about the potential of and the difficulties in working in grassroots organizing. I had to start from scratch in the neighbourhood and train students to do the work. One of the first things that students had to learn was that they were not doing social work in any of the ways that they had been taught in the classroom. They were out there at peoples' doors to promote an idea of social change through participation in a local organizing effort. Individual change (casework) was not part of the program. Once they got that idea, it was easier to move ahead. The process channelled the discontent that residents were feeling into organizing. There was always a tension between what people felt and what they were willing to do. Perhaps it was the times (mid-1970s) and the actual conditions that contributed to peoples' willingness to invite you into their homes and discuss the problems, however, this did not necessarily translate into action. There were times when a student would tell me that she/he had talked to many people on a block and expected twenty-five at the first meeting. The reality was more often five or six. Peoples' willingness to participate in local action is shaped by a variety of factors such as their own energy levels and time commitments—working-class jobs, children, and so on. Many believed that nothing could be accomplished, and others hoped that they would move out of the neighbourhood. Further, gender shaped the organizing effort. The neighbourhood was viewed as an extension of the home and the issues tended to attract more women than men. For women, taking on a public persona as leaders created tensions at home and their activities were at times discouraged by their husbands.

The process of mobilization is difficult; it takes time and investment in people. But it is possible. This is the central lesson and one that I still carry. Mobilization is a key element; without it there is little that an organization can do. There are two good reasons for this. The first is that the power of an organization to win issues is built on numbers of people. Second, in the process of participating in local struggles, people gain awareness, build solidarity with others, and create democratic opportunities. Community organizing can contribute to social change by mobilizing people to act for their own interest in an organized way. When I look back, the most effective efforts have always occurred through mobilization. Perhaps the most discouraging change in the community movement is that this seems to have been forgotten. More and more, organizations represent people—or at least claim that they do—but they do not try to capture the spirit that is present in the process of organizing when people speak and act on their own behalves.

I have critical comments and questions about this experience. The period of effective organizing was short—a few years. The kind of work we were doing is hard to sustain. It is not easy, particularly now, to find support for the type of organizing that we were doing. Funding bodies do not like to support projects and efforts that are "political," meaning those that overtly challenge the status quo by organizing people directly. Such efforts cannot be easily controlled. Given these difficulties we did find some success, but in retrospect there are lessons that can be learned by raising some critical issues. The question of organization is central. I will discuss this question in the chapters that follow. For now, I want to raise a doubt that bothered me at the time. We spent a lot of time and energy on organizational maintenance. Our small neighbourhood groups would often hold numerous meetings every month, including block meetings, coordinating committee meetings with representatives from each block, committee meetings that were focused on specific issues, leadership meetings, as well as weekly meetings of the organizing team. The structure provided stability and what appeared to be a democratic, transparent process of decision-making, but it took a toll. There were not many leaders and after a while they were spending more time in meetings than in any other part of the process.

The impact was similar for organizers. An organizer must work on recruitment. It is *the* most important task. When the demands of organizational maintenance become too great, recruitment does not occur and the organization does not grow. Thus, the lesson for me is that building organization implies the creation of simple, flexible structures that allow new recruits and leaders to enter. I think that organization is necessary, but it is easy for a stagnant organization to hide behind a stable structure. The processes we participated in were dynamic when they were working well. The tension is between putting in place an organizational form that is transparent and open versus one that takes over the time and energy of those involved for internal processes. With this experience, I have begun to believe that for organizing to go beyond short-term initiatives requires stable and flexible structures, whose day-to-day maintenance does not displace the task of mobilization. I will return to this point throughout the book, but I raise it here because I think there is a lot of confusion about the concepts of community organization and community organizing. The latter is about a process not necessarily reproducing the weight of organization. Further, as one puts in place more formal organizations and structures, funds are required to support staff and operating expenses. Fundraising can become the driving force of organizational life rather than the pursuit of its goals and mission. Even in the 1970s, when securing funds for innovative activities was relatively easier, this was an issue. As organizations grew there were greater demands for money, which could distort the goals of the organization either because of the time and energy devoted to these ends or because the money received was linked to the priorities of the funder and not the organization itself.

Over the years, I have thought a lot about the role of community organizers, particularly their accountability and their influence in local groups. Organizers are outsiders. I experienced this sharply in my door-to-door encounters. I was young (at the time), educated, and male while many who were prepared to become active had not had access to a lot of formal education, were women with young children, or worked in menial jobs. Because of who I was I had influence and some power. In addition, I had worked in organizing before, and had a pretty good idea of the type of work I was doing. The relationship was not equal. It also took a while to build trust. Why should an organizer be trusted? We are asking people to behave differently in relations of authority—to challenge their landlords, fight city hall. However, organizing is not manipulation. People ultimately vote with their feet. An organizer has no rewards or benefits to give out; taking part is voluntary. If residents attend meetings and participate in the process it is because they have become convinced of the merits of the work and because they have cemented a relationship with the organizer.

Having argued this, it is also important to acknowledge that organizers have power. They can shape agendas and pick and support leaders. I have come to believe that there is little one can do about this relationship; it is there. Community organizers do facilitate and stimulate local processes that would not have happened otherwise. It is important, however, to recognize their roles and their power. As an organization grows, leadership has to be encouraged to challenge organizers and continue to make them accountable. This relationship changes over time. In the beginning it is usually the organizer that has a lot of power. With the transition to the latter stage, when an organizing structure has been put in place, the role of the organizer should shift and become more like a staff member accountable to the membership. This shift is central and should allow leaders and members to strengthen their voices. The role of the organizer and her/his power and role are inevitable, and the difficult questions that it raises need to be confronted. These are not easily resolved. If a community organization is in practice a democratic opportunity, a place in which active participation of its members can become a possibility, then organizers have to learn to live the tensions around their own power and authority and learn to actively shift control to members and leaders.

Another troubling question was the relationship of this type of neighbourhood organizing to wider processes of social change. By the end of the 1970s there was a strong Marxist-Leninist movement in Quebec. There were major divisions in this movement with several Maoist tendencies. These political groups had attracted many young, politicized activists who brought their politics into factories and the community movement. They promoted and deepened class analysis, drawing on the legacies of Marxism, but their style and authoritarian form of organization alienated many of the working class that they were trying to recruit. I began to accept their analysis along with some of the Marxist scholarly work that was reborn in universities. On the other hand, I rejected the authoritarianism of this movement. The group around Parallel Institute believed that we were organizing people in the English-speaking working class who would participate in a wider working-class movement in Quebec. In retrospect, this was certainly naive and inaccurate. Further, the people we were organizing did not buy any of it. They were able to understand interest and power and how these relations affected them in their neighbourhoods and workplaces, as well as how capitalism created poverty and unhealthy living conditions. But they didn't believe in the rhetoric of the "far left." They wanted the gains that can be made through organizing—such as better housing and neighbourhood conditions.

From a Marxist perspective, then, the primary class contradictions would be played out in factories through the struggles at the point of production. Work in the community was secondary. These ideas created doubt about the potential of local work. So, what was the role of community organizing in terms of promoting social change? The way I try to answer this question has remained relatively consistent over the years. Fundamentally, the core for me is power, and organizing is the means of creating a collective voice and allowing a group to shape events that touch its members' lives. There is a danger here, and this is one challenge that Marxism raised. What is this voice for? Is it necessarily progressive? Does it ally itself with working-class and later feminist struggles? Here the answer is no. We have certainly seen right-wing groups using the lessons of organizing to promote their positions and to make demands on the state. There has to be another dimension—ideology and/or values, and here we are treading on a path strewn with obstacles. The organizing that I was doing in the 1970s was shaped by goals such as increasing social and economic equality and extending democracy. But we live in a society that teaches that inequality is inevitable and deserved and that most people are uninformed so they really are not capable of making decisions. Further, selecting between political parties on a regular basis is what democracy is all about. The challenge is to move from the day-to-day of organizing to promoting ideology without imposing it. The Marxists put this on the table, and they used community organizations as forums for political education—promoting their own political line while ignoring the immediate interests of the group. In some ways this undermined the effectiveness of organizing and in some instances the Marxists were kicked out. There is a necessary balance between maintaining concrete struggles in which people can learn to work collectively, and building power while raising the broader political and social questions. The lesson of that period was that both were needed along with a solid dose of alliance-building in order to broaden the local into a wider vision of social change. It is here that we need to work—the balance. It is the central challenge, keeping one eye on winning local, concrete struggles and the other eye on the broader picture, building bridges with the wider struggles. The organizer has to understand that for people to be involved in local work there has to be something in it for them. At the same time, he/she has an educational role to play that goes beyond the experience and begins to link it to wider social and political movements. I will now turn to an experience in a social movement in order to see the type of politics that were missing in local work. I will also present an indirect contrast of organizing processes.

## PEACE MOVEMENT ACTIVITIES

The early and mid-1980s was a period of intense activity in the peace and disarmament movement. The United States had raised the stakes in the nuclear arms race and its rhetoric against the former Soviet Union. Not to be outdone, the latter became a weaker mirror image of the former. The two at times seemed to be in an irrational death struggle with most of humanity as collateral damage. However, the most dramatic occurrences did not come from the super powers with their positioning and escalation, but from the massive opposition to it. I will not enter into an analysis of the arms race and the politics of the period. But it forms a backdrop to the very important personal and political lessons about the role of organizing within a social movement and some of the challenges and opportunities that were provided through that experience. Further, there is a continuity between these movements and those that organized the mobilization of more recent movements.

I became active in the peace movement through my connections with the magazine *Our Generation*, which had its origins in the movement for nuclear disarmament during the 1960s. Through one of its editors, I became a member of a group called Academics for Nuclear Disarmament, which had produced a statement alerting the public to the dangers of the arms race. I found that, typical of the peace movement, there were many people with good intentions but little skill or capacity for the organization of public protest and mobilization. At the same time, there was a strong public sentiment and support for disarmament. The movement brought together a variety of political traditions and orientations. In Canada, the main campaign was against cruise missile testing. The broad-based movement did not stop the testing, but it did have a different impact. As opposed to community organizations that work for specific gains, social movements change popular understanding through campaigns; they redefine the common-sense understanding of the issues. Thus, the idea of nuclear weapons was thoroughly discredited, as was even the divides of East/West; in this way, the premise of the Cold War was challenged.

The period was a rich one for me. I was involved with a wide variety of groups working in the disarmament movement, and there was a positive and exciting energy within them. I was proud of the fact that I had played a role in a disarmament demonstration with estimates of 30,000 people who formed a human chain between the Soviet and the U.S. embassies. This demonstration was a point of convergence for many political actors, ranging from feminists to ecologists, trade unions, and a variety of lefties of all stripes. This type of convergence is rare but joining together for common campaigns creates a climate of optimism and a space for politics that can be done differently. There were, however, divisions. On the tactical side, there were those who believed that civil disobedience and getting arrested was the only morally legitimate tactic, while others wanted to appeal to a majority who would be attracted to more traditional means of protest. Ideologically, there were divisions between those who supported the Soviet Union and groups that I was working with that argued for a policy of non-alignment. There were those who wanted the positions of the peace movement to be shaped by a more radical ideology and a longer-term vision of social change and those who saw it as a single issue. These were some of the many complexities. For this discussion, it is the lessons for community organizing that are important.

The significant contrast for me between community organization and participation in the peace movement was the form of organization. The former tends to involve a clear structure with specific roles for staff, members, and volunteers. While there are peace and disarmament organizations, the peace movement is by definition decentralized with many centres of activity. Spontaneity of action in unexpected places creates the sense of the movement. Also, the way that issues and actions touch people in places where there is not a specific organization contributes to the breadth and convergence of its participants. For example, teachers brought peace issues into the classroom, unionists talked about military conversion to civilian production, women organized peace camps, and students and professors confronted issues of military research on campuses. Can this type of convergence be consciously reproduced or is it more about a specific period and events? I believe that these moments are important but they cannot be "organized." Rather, they come about because of small efforts in many places to keep ideas alive, sustain action in general, and bring new analyses of events to public awareness. The peace movement was not a spontaneous departure; it grew out of other social and political movements and reflected how they had achieved a sophisticated organizational capacity and readiness to engage with a wider public. Each new round of activity contributed positive and negative lessons about how to go forward to the next round of the struggle.

Trusting diversity and decentralization is a key element of movements on any level. In community organizations, we are taught to put together tightly organized events. The peace movement did that, too. For example, the human chain described above was the product of many months of planning, mobilization, and education. At the same time, many events and new forms of activity sprang up in unaffiliated groups. Movement forms are by definition loose and chaotic. Attempts at centralization often occur after the blossoming of the local and usually fail or demobilize. I was part of a group that tried to put together a province-wide organization of non-aligned peace groups, but it never came to much. The activity centres, represented by these groups, were just that, and they did not have long-term expectations and agendas. By the time a broad-based organization was in place, the peak of the mobilization and popular support had passed. Meetings became routine, providing little in the way of excitement and energy. There is a delicate balance between the necessity of coordination and imposing an organization form on movement activities. This was an important lesson for me, and it supports my belief that large mobilizations are short-term and cannot be shaped by traditional types of organization. One has to go with the energy of the movement, bring political perspectives into it, and contribute to alliance-building, but the movement will run its course. I think that in community organizing, we spend too much time on putting structures in place and too little time on the actions that create and support a spirit of movement and opposition.

Practices of working by consensus were an important element of the processes in the peace movement. We did not only oppose a range of issues related to peace, but we did it in ways that challenged hierarchy and domination. The most overt practice was consensus decision-making. This came to our groups mainly from the women's movement. There was conflict about this practice. Some argued in a principled way for it, while others did not want to waste time on the arduous process of building consensus. I participated in many meetings that were slowed by a difficult process of arriving at decisions we all were able to accept. A vote would have been faster but those on the losing side would have not have had their voices heard in the same way. I liked the process but saw some flaws in it. Consensus decision-making implied that those participating in the decision had a shared core of beliefs. Decisions, therefore, were premised on common assumptions. Consensus can work in those situations if there is openness to working out an agreement on specific aspects of the work that does not compromise any core values. In broad-based ad hoc arrangements such as the peace movement, core beliefs were never discussed beyond acceptance of the specific campaign. Consensus was difficult when people from diverse political and social backgrounds came together to organize a specific event or campaign.

We experimented with process in other ways. In public meetings, women remarked that men spoke more frequently than they did. In order to ameliorate this situation, we passed a rule that there would be an alternation between men and women speakers, particularly in public meetings. This did have a positive effect and reduced the dominant role that men often played in these forums. Affinity groups were organized as a means to prepare for direct action. These groups were part of wider campaigns and they worked by occupying or blocking entrances to government and/or corporate offices. They were small groups who trained together for this act of non-violent civil disobedience. These actions were prepared through coordination between these groups. Affinity groups were democratically organized and worked on the principles of consensus decision-making. It was not only the way that they functioned that interested me, but also the way they created a decentralized approach to direct action. This tradition is an old one that goes back to many different campaigns and draws on Gandhi's principles of non-violence. The long legacy of protest and creative disruption continues. The key lesson here is how the process is intertwined with outcomes. Social movements of our time are implicitly challenging the limits of parliamentary democracy and are arguing that a broader voice has to be heard. However, at the same time, new democratic practices need to be constructed in practice so that the processes of building protest can include the voices of those involved and reduce the influence of traditional forms of leadership.

Perhaps the most important lesson was the complex interaction of the global and the local. The slogan "think globally, act locally" has become little more than a cliché. In fact, it is the key element in a new practice that has paved the way for the social movements against globalization of recent times. However, the slogan is incorrect because thinking globally should imply acting beyond the local. The escalation of the arms race was a problem that was far removed from the neighbourhoods and the institutions in which we organized, but each level of the movement—and the links of solidarity between social movements—was the basis of the success of the 1980s peace movement. It was able to discredit both the arms race and the polarization of the East and the West with its diverse actions and campaigns. At the local level, for example, I was part of a neighbourhood group that conducted an independent popular referendum to declare our district a nuclear-free zone. We had no formal authority and what we did had no legal weight, but we reached hundreds of people through education and the voting process itself, and were part of a larger coalition that pressured the city of Montreal into declaring itself nuclear-free. These gestures were largely symbolic but it created the momentum for a larger challenge.

At the same time as the work was going on "from below," there were new forms of international networking taking place. Internationalism grew on the momentum of local action and stimulated it as well. I was fortunate to attend the European Nuclear Disarmament Convention in Amsterdam in 1985. There were activists from all over Europe and America building their analyses and sharing strategies in an atmosphere of solidarity. I was witnessing internationalism in practice. Those events demonstrated the necessity of linking the local with the global but in ways that were concrete and specific. The presence of an international movement acts to stimulate local action. I think that some of the renewed activism that is confronting the processes of globalization today is built on the patterns established in the peace movement: local autonomy, decentralized structures, effective communication that facilitates shared analysis, and perspectives that contribute to the building of internationalist practice.

The period in the peace movement was a very rich one for me. Perhaps this was sustained by the fact that it was broadly based and involved people from a wide variety of backgrounds and interests. I often meet people who were politically active in that period (the early 1980s) and there is a strong sense of personal friendship that has been gained from doing politics in an atmosphere of personal and political solidarity. At the same time, I do not want to idealize the experience; there were conflicts, both political and personal. These are inevitable in an open movement. For most of us, the work was voluntary and pushed into our personal lives; we were required to balance jobs, childcare responsibilities, and relationships with the demands of the movement. These were part of it all—learning to live your politics with the reality of your life. That challenge was one that provoked personal growth and reflection.

I also had questions and doubts. One tension for me was between my background as a community organizer and my role as a movement activist. The former teaches two things that conflict with the latter. First, an organizer tries to balance his/her ideology and values with the demands for group cohesion. Thus, almost by definition, compromises are made. In the context of a social movement, it is more permissible and often necessary to polarize questions even if it appears to be divisive. The question of non-alignment was an example of this dilemma. Many in the peace movement had fallen into an uncomfortable alliance with pro-Soviet forces that were led internationally by the World Peace Council. Others opposed this organization for tactical and more fundamental reasons. I will not go into the arguments here except to state that we were not interested in reproducing Cold War hysteria, but we wanted to oppose the escalating, reciprocal nature of the arms race. In addition, the support of the independent peace movements that emerged in Eastern bloc countries was another source of conflict. The position of some was that these issues should be ignored for the sake of unity. Those of us supporting a non-aligned perspective thought that unity would have been created falsely and that an alternative vision that went "beyond the blocs" was a starting point. The debate put me in a new role as a partisan of a position and not as an organizer who pursued consensus and unity. Further, I began to feel more strongly that it was important to bring vision and explicit politics into an organizing process. There is an inevitable tension between how much and how far, and the balancing of vision and engagement with diversity. Without vision and explicit politics, the possibility of basic social change is lost, but at the same time it is impossible to mobilize large numbers if one remains sectarian.

The second issue was organization-building versus the style and forms of organization in a social movement. Community organizing is premised on the assumption that building a relatively permanent structure with clear processes for the delegation of power and roles facilitates longevity and democracy. Social movements, by definition, tend to be much looser. Groups mobilize for specific campaigns or actions and then disband. Some organizations continue but play an educational and more traditional lobbying function. They are buoyed during specific periods of mass mobilization. It is impossible to impose a structure on a movement. There can be organizations that grow out of the movement but they will not sustain the mass mobilization; that part is time-limited. Social movements are short-lived and cannot be reproduced or channelled into traditional organizations. The role of activists is to support and contribute to the specific events and campaigns, bringing critical politics and debate into them, but they should not expect that the movement as such can be organized. One final comment: despite the reservations and questions that I have raised about neighbourhood organizing and the peace movement, the spirit of these activities was optimistic. The revolution did not happen, but I felt that there were victories; new leadership was supported, political consciousness was promoted, and in general there was a sense that social change was possible through both neighbourhood and social movement organizing. However, in the years that followed, the context shifted.

## CHANGING DIRECTION—COMMUNITY ORGANIZING REDEFINED

My involvement in the peace movement and other activities had taken me out of community organizations. It was not until the mid-1980s that I started to become involved again, and I found some discouraging changes. In addition, the context and the debate had both shifted. The context was shaped by two factors. Unemployment had risen in a way that was unprecedented since the depression of the 1930s. Factory closures with massive layoffs were daily occurrences in working-class neighbourhoods. The changes were part of a deindustrialization that faced many cities. The consequences were high levels of poverty, and for many young people the possibilities of work seemed remote. The second factor was the restructuring of the role of the state. The welfare state was cut back, but more fundamentally there was an ideological shift. The state would no longer be the primary social provider; the market and the community were to share the responsibility. New relationships between the community and the government were in place. Community organizations were pressured into partnership with government and innovative solutions were sought in order to confront the crisis.

I was involved in two projects. The first was in the organizing committee for and subsequently as a member of the executive of a community council in my own district. The second was in community economic development (CED). These examples represent general shifts in community work and I found them to be discouraging, despite their potential. These themes are central to this book; therefore, in this section, I will sketch out the basic elements from a personal point of view. The most striking shift, particularly after participating in peace movement activities, was the lack of mobilization. Community organizations represented and advocated on behalf of their members or clients. There were a few instances of attempts to mobilize, but these seemed to me to be half-hearted and not systematic. The change was striking. It had not been that many years before that we as organizers had insisted on the basic premise that one had to reach "the people," and in order to do this, one had to spend time in the peoples' homes and other places where they congregated. Organizing was about bringing people together, helping them to have a voice, and representing one's own interests. Instead, I found politically progressive professionals who believed that they could represent people, and they defined this as the best path in working for social change. In doing so, however, they lost their base and some of their legitimacy.

Another shift was expressed through community organizations developing different services. There was a range of politics associated with them. Some were innovative and creative, finding new and experimental ways to respond to social problems (for example, training businesses); some embodied the values and politics of the social movement activists that started them (for example, women's shelters); and some were traditional charities (for example, food banks). I will discuss these shifts in detail in a later chapter. The point for me was that the community sector seemed to be politically in a dead end. It had become competent and professionalized, had gradually negotiated recognition from the government, and in many instances had secured recurring funding arrangements. The relationship with the state was complex. On the one hand, there was an element of conflict on the status of these new services and other social policies; on the other, there was collaboration and new partnership between government and community. The politics were complex—and unclear. But one thing was sure: there was little at the grassroots as community organizations stood between the people and the state in some kind of mediating or advocating relationship. I saw this relationship played out in the community council. It became an organization of organizations as most of the community organizations became members. We campaigned for improvements and contributed to some of the local improvements such as the building of a swimming pool and an enlarged recreation centre. However, public meetings were rare in those campaigns, and the leadership fell into the hands of professionals.

Another new form of activism became in vogue in this period—community economic development (CED). I fell into it, rather than seeking it out. It seemed to me that the integration of economic development into the community had potential, and that was what attracted me. I believed that the split between the social and the economic had been one of the limits of community organizing. For the next ten years I was a member of various boards of directors and working groups in CED organizations; as well, through research projects and writing I was able to learn a lot about it. I had maintained a critical stance towards it at that point, acknowledging a limited potential for social change and at the same time its dangers. The potential of CED, like any other community project, is in its ability to create democratic opportunities and to help people find ways to gain power. The dangers were the ideology that it co-promoted with its government funders and representatives of big business that small-scale and individual enterprise was a solution to the growing crisis of work that had been prominent since the mid-1980s. Some CED was initiated at the local level through coalitions of social actors such as communities, unions, and businesses as a way to respond to the economic devastation of the period. In Montreal, after several of these grassroots efforts had gained a foothold and received funding, the city, provincial, and federal governments saw this as a useful strategy to promote local economic development. In addition, the organizations established became para-governmental with narrow definitions of their mandates. In some ways, these new organizations set up new ruling relations at the local level as they administered prepackaged government programs, particularly those aimed at integrating the unemployed into the labour market. I witnessed these changes and within one of the organizations I pushed for a strategy that would be more active in the promotion of an economic vision for the district and would include public hearings. These never happened because the leadership of the organization would not step out of the predetermined program packages imposed by their funding agencies. I have been discouraged by these processes and feel that CED practice in Montreal has been rapidly institutionalized. At the same time, there is potential in the CED movement, particularly in grassroots initiatives that have put democratic workplaces in place. There are also some examples of CED organizations that have promoted alternative perspectives on local development that take into account low-cost housing, job creation, and public participation in the process. It is the underlying belief in small business development, the entrepreneurial spirit, that I question the most. In some CED organizations, there is little promotion of a collective vision. Effort is put into organizing support for business development, such as access to credit and technical resources. The emphasis becomes an individual or small business model. I have described this as "trickling sideways," as there are few benefits except to the small group that sets up the business. At the same time, it promotes an ideology that small business development can compensate for high levels of poverty. I do not believe this; it is like using micro-tools to fix macro-problems. Because of the emphasis on small business development, because of its technocratic/administrative face, and most important because it has not (with a couple of exceptions) engaged the wider community in a political and social process, I decided to leave the board and executive of the CED organization.

I felt that the period of the 1980s and 1990s had created a community sector rather than a community movement. Its orientation was shaped by a professionally controlled service orientation. It had become, for me, an outgrowth of the state with little autonomy or vision of social change. I was out of step and in meetings I often felt profoundly alienated. I had seen the community organizing go from "adolescence," with the anger, hope, and energy that implied, to "adulthood," which meant compliance and acceptance of a "responsible" role within the social order. There were ongoing challenges and continuity with the more contentious past but these were in the minority and did not have a lot of success in mobilizing citizens.

## ATTEMPTS AT RENEWAL

I returned to grassroots neighbourhood organizing. It was an experience that for a while renewed my optimism about the prospect for community organizing. An old friend approached me to help him with a new organizing initiative in a low-income, multicultural neighbourhood in Montreal. I won't go into all of the details and all of the mistakes and problems (there were many!), but I will start with the positive highlights. The main attraction for me was the commitment to a grassroots process that would mobilize people and set up a local organization. I saw this as an opportunity for a renewal of practice.

When the opportunity arose to return to a grassroots process, I felt that it was timely and personally challenging. It was a return to many of my earlier experiences. The process began with hope. My role was as an educator and an unpaid consultant. I was able to present workshops on topics such as, "What is organizing?" and "How to negotiate." I met with citizens from the area and a small group of youth who were being trained to work as local organizers. There was an ongoing process of outreach through knocking on doors, talking about specific conditions such as housing, crime, and traffic. There were actions—sometimes spontaneous. For example, a young single mother, who had just become involved, picketed an intersection with a couple of friends and children, demanding that drivers slow down and respect traffic signs. Gradually, citizens formed themselves into a group, nominated some leaders, and spoke for the neighbourhood. This was a good beginning, a hopeful start. For me, it was fun to watch people who had rarely had a voice be able to come forward and begin to play an active role in shaping their neighbourhood.

However, there were problems at many levels. One was the jealousy of other local organizations that felt they had a mandate to represent the interests of the residents and were uncomfortable about the fact that residents wanted their own voice. This tension was played out through direct conflict with the person who initiated the project and the withholding of support when the new group approached funding sources. However, there were some crucial errors made in the organizing that led to a replication of some of the worst characteristics of other community groups. As the group evolved, a leader came forward who was powerful, dynamic, and fundamentally anti-democratic. She would not tolerate any criticism or internal debate. There was little place for anyone else except people who passively accepted her role. Further, one of the tactics used by the organization was to invite the mayor during his re-election campaign in 1998 to spend a weekend in the neighbourhood to "see how the other half [more like 85 per cent] lives." The mayor was down in the polls and faced the prospects of a defeat. His visit turned his campaign around as he transformed himself into a populist. He subsequently won. This tactic put the group on the map and gave it a huge boost in its public image and legitimacy, particularly with the city administration. However, rather than using the event as a tactic, the group became more drawn into the political process and became viewed by others in the community as an uncritical ally of the mayor and his party. One of the rewards was to receive funding from a new municipal program. However, at the same time, the victory further isolated the group from the rest of the community organizations.

The group secured a minimum of funding and opened a storefront. But the tension continued and grew. The grassroots activities diminished, and people spent time in the storefront arguing among themselves and trying to parlay their alliance with the city into more secure funding. Periodically there was outreach and attempts to broaden the organizational base by recruiting interested residents, but there was no room for new members within the organization. My role continued through this process. I met with a core group one morning every second week. The group was made up of staff and some of the more active board members. We discussed what should be done, planned campaigns, and examined ways to develop skills that could be used in the organizing process. Yet nothing happened, and I began to spend more and more time mediating conflicts. The final straw for me was the collaboration of the leader of the organization with a city staff member on a plan to provide funds for community organizations. The process was undemocratic and provoked opposition from many of the groups and community leaders that I had known and worked with in other capacities. I was able to support the opposition by providing a secret first draft of the program. It became clear that the goal of the leader of the organization and the small group around her was to secure funds regardless of the political costs. I decided at that point to leave the organization.

This experience provoked reflection about the limits and possibilities of grassroots organizing. There were many questions and unresolved issues for me. The processes at the community level were highly professional and were cut off from the traditions of social activism. I have met many who support the newer approaches, and I find their self-congratulatory tone irritating. Is it a question of my age, or my inability to accept the changes in the world around me? I wonder if what I had hoped for community organizing is no longer possible. Maybe the optimism of the earlier periods cannot be replicated and I have to try to find the elements within current practice that can be used to promote opposition and democratic processes. There is a lot of discussion about social/political/economic determinants, but we have to understand the role of agency in the process—how we each shape practice and use opportunities. It is easy to fall into deterministic assumptions. But practice is never uniform; there are always cracks in the dominant form and examples of grassroots challenges to those with power. It is this tension that shapes the opportunities. We as activists and organizers have to learn to seize and to support these periods to strengthen the movement of social and political opposition, and we also have to learn to recognize them. Perhaps this is the most difficult part.

To find these spaces we need to consider the two intertwining factors of agency and context. As an activist, the perspectives and ideologies that I carry with me were shaped in the period of my own political and social awakening. I think that is key for me. It shapes a vision, a stance, and a political orientation. These were born in a particular time in which the social movements were stronger and the opportunities greater. The context has shifted. There are fewer opportunities and the openings are narrower, but they exist. The restructuring of the economy and the state I discussed above should not be read as the beginning of the end for community organization's role in providing opposition to government and the wider system of globalized capitalism. The current period is creating a renewed opposition, but it is outside of the community level. It is in social movements often led by young activists, and it directly confronts corporate power on the world stage. The question for me is whether these new activist activities will have an impact on the community sector and shake it up.

Community organizing does not exist in a vacuum. It is stimulated by the social and political movements of each historical period. When I look back to my earlier periods of activity, these included the student movement and counterculture of the 1960s and 1970s in Canada, and the civil rights movement in the United States. Later, it was the women's movement and the peace, ecology, and identity movements that stimulated the founding of a variety of community organizations. These were founded alongside those that provided traditional and innovative services. Some organizations stimulated by social movements, at least in their early stages, continued to struggle in opposition. They brought democratic processes into the workplace; they challenged professionalism and hierarchies and continued to battle for social justice, either as advocates or through direct mobilization. Over the years that followed, often because of a weakening of the social movements, because of an isolation of the community organization, or because of the pressures of the demands of their funders, most of these initiatives lost their radical politics and became professionally driven service providers.

I think that there is an uneasy relationship and tension between social movements and community organizations. By definition, social movements are unstable. They tend to be relatively short-lived, but they create activists. In writing the second edition of this book, I notice a parallel to the first one. At the time of the first edition, there was an upsurge of activism and organizing against the international shift to global capitalism and free trade. Many young people found themselves politically engaged for the first time in their lives. I had the privilege of interviewing some younger activists who are beginning to take their place and find ways to involve themselves in social change activities. It was encouraging to listen to their stories, analysis, and a description of their activities. They had learned political and social awareness, plus skills and knowledge about how to engage in struggle. The campaigns are training grounds. At the time I questioned whether the new activists would find a place within community organizations, what kind of openness there would be for them, and what kind of challenge they would bring. The answers are complex; many have become involved in a variety of local community organizations and international development projects and bring an analysis formed by the "anti-globalization" movement into their roles and jobs. Others have stayed on the outside and formed new initiatives based on their radical politics. The Immigrant Workers Centre that I will discuss in detail in the last chapter has some organizers from the younger generation who have brought their perspectives but who have also learned from older organizers, particularly immigrants who continue the struggles from their home countries. As I am writing, I see the student movement in some ways as similar to the wave protest in the late 1990s and early 2000s, insofar as it excited and politicized a new generation of activists and organizers. Hopefully, many from this generation will carry forward their experiences and insights and continue in the struggle for economic and social justice.

This brings me to the present and this book. It is my project of reflection and analysis. I think it is important to try to understand some of the lessons I have derived over the past forty years; to look at some of the constants as well as some of the innovations or variations on the themes; and to enter into a political dialogue and critique. I think it is important not only to look back, but also to look forward. I have organized the book accordingly. The themes and questions I have outlined from my own experience will be the basis of the exploration. The main theme will be the contribution of community organizing to the process of social change. There are some definitions that are needed that have been implicit above. For me, social change can be understood by the use of the concepts such as democracy, redistribution, power, resistance, opposition, and critical analysis.

The book examines these processes beginning with a general chapter that presents definitions, models, and some theoretical perspectives that inform the different forms of community action. Chapter 2 presents a historical overview of community organizing with a couple of case studies that reflect its changes. The third chapter looks back to examine the origins of the social action approach and its legacies and contributions. I have also added a new chapter on contemporary examples to demonstrate its continuity. The fifth chapter looks at the shifts that took place after the 1980s and its problems, limits, and opportunities. The concluding chapter is new. I examine in more detail the practice of the Immigrant Workers Centre that I helped found twelve years ago and where I am currently based (there is life after academia). I use this experience to explore some of the complex challenges of organizing in the current period. The second part of the book pulls together the themes and the questioning. Personally, I find that questions are easy to raise, but it is only through practice that we can begin to find directions—and only if we work together with others who share in our analysis and struggle together for the same goals of change based on social and economic justice. I am fortunate to have such a group at the Immigrant Workers Centre.

# CHAPTER ONE

# THEORETICAL PERSPECTIVES AND MODELS OF COMMUNITY WORK

Community organizing practice has rich traditions. It begins with experiences in the real world. This engagement is the motor that drives it. At the same time, theory and models can be useful as guides. There is a healthy tension between the two worlds—and this is not easily resolved. In this chapter, I will outline theoretical positions and models of practice. The goal is to draw on these approaches to help understand practice and be more explicit about its underpinnings. This chapter will not be a literature review, but I have selectively drawn on the literature in order to come to grips with practice questions. In this chapter, I will cover values and theory as well as practice models.

The difficulty I face with this task is that, by its very nature, community organizing begins with the complexities of practice. Creating the processes that can lead to changes in peoples' lives is a daunting task, to say the least. It requires skills, long hours, perseverance, and—out of necessity—pragmatism. Trade-offs are part of the day-to-day reality. The basic values and theoretical perspectives of the organizers can be lost in the fast-moving realities of development and struggle. Yet, at the same time, the existing theories and models—despite the fact that they do not easily connect to the "real world" of social and political engagement—can contribute to our analysis and vision. Further, the forces that shape practice do not come from either texts or the practitioner. More often they are structured by the wider political and economic contexts, which in turn can shape the availability of support and the issues faced by organizations. In other words, the organizers have to play the game of finding support for their activities within the existing boundaries and structures, yet without compromising their political goals and vision. This process has a major impact on practice by pushing those in the field to believe that pragmatism and compromise can be the only guiding values. At best, there are tensions between these forces that shape the initiatives and the ideas that guide them. At times, however, there is little reflection on practice, and without reflection practice can become limited by the resources available to carry out a program of activities. I believe that without critical reflection there is a profound political danger. We are doomed to fall into patterns defined by those with resources and in the process lose our vision—what we were trying to do in the first place. Therefore, this chapter will try to make explicit those aspects that are often lost in the day-to-day—the complex interconnections between values and theory and the models of community organizing.

There is a particular tension that I face in bridging the worlds of practice and the university. My role as a teacher and a researcher pushes me towards trying to find perspectives that can contribute to an understanding and an analysis of practice. In order to teach it, I am required to discern patterns of practice and present theory that helps students to analyze it. At the same time, I am pushed both by my own involvement in the field as well as the demands of students to bring the discussion down to earth and face the question of how theory and models contribute to the everyday demands of practice. This challenge to balance the two is one that is enriching and difficult. But there are fundamental issues that go beyond either the immediacy of practice or an academic stance towards it. I keep returning to the nagging question that is at the core of this book—what does community organizing contribute to the process of social change? This is not an academic question, but it is the issue on which all the other questions turn. This is the question that I always come back to. It is the question in a way that haunts those of us on the left who have looked to community organizing as one vehicle that can promote social justice, reshape power relations, challenge the privilege of the few, and create a voice for the powerless. Fundamentally, I ask that community organizing contribute to the process of opposition in our society and resist capitalism, patriarchy, racism, and environmental destruction! Practice needs to be grounded in the day-to-day struggles and at the same time carry a notion of the longer term and a critical social and economic analysis. Both pragmatism and vision are necessary. Without the former there will not be participation of citizens in action; without the latter, we are condemned to be travelling without maps, never knowing where we will end up. In the material that follows I will keep in mind the tension between the visions of social change and pragmatic engagements in the field as I explore the traditions of community organizing. Historical material and examples will be provided as the starting point. These examples will be used as a place to begin looking at the models, theories, and underlying values of community organizing.

## DEFINITIONS

Providing a definition of community organizing is a necessary first step. Rubin and Rubin (1992) provide a useful starting point. They argue:

> Community organizing is a search for social power and an effort to combat perceived helplessness through learning that what appears personal is often political. (p. 1)

and

> Community organizing creates a capacity for democracy and for sustained social change. It can make society more adaptable and governments more accountable.... Community organizing means bringing people together to combat shared problems and to increase their say about decisions that affect their lives. (p. 3)

Several elements are important in this statement. The first is "social power," which stands in contrast to "perceived helplessness." Social power is gained through collective action. Here is the core of organizing. We will see in this book how power is used in different ways.

One tradition—community action—sees power as a way to push others to do something about group needs such as housing or neighbourhood improvements. The other tradition—personal development—is based on the power to do something for oneself through collective action. This can include self-help or building local institutions for social or economic provision. The next concept introduced by Rubin and Rubin is that of learning. The authors focus on the movement from the personal to the political. Learning, which is a participatory process that teaches about how power operates and what can be done to advance one's interests, is essential in all processes of organizing. Through these processes, individuals can develop many skills and learn to become leaders. Thus, these processes constitute one of the underlying currents in community organizing that contributes to both personal and social change.

"Capacity for democracy" is another key element in the above definition. Democracy has to be understood in the widest sense possible. It is a process of people gaining control of aspects of their own lives through the organizations in which they have a voice. This is in contrast to the dominant notion of democracy, which is limited to periodic voting and participation in the electoral process. Through community organizing, people can learn to shape decisions in organizations that touch their lives and to exert pressure in order to create responsiveness from the different levels of government. Democratic practice at the local level is one of the most important contributions of community organizing. It is both an outcome and an ongoing process. However, one central question is the breadth of its influence. There are many successes locally; in them citizens have created democratic organizations, enlarged opportunities for participation, and influenced local decision-making. However, determining whether these processes have translated into a more democratic society is problematic. The contradiction we face is that the strong central authorities in our society, which are controlled either by private corporate interests or their allies in traditional political parties, provide few opportunities for democratic accountability to the wider population, while at the same time there are local institutions supporting a voice for people. Moving from the local to the state or to corporate power is the core challenge—in it we see the limits of organizing in shaping democratic processes in the wider society, another one of those tensions implicit in examining the connections between community organizing and social change.

Finally, Rubin and Rubin introduce "sustained social change" as an outcome. This perhaps is the most difficult aspect of the definition. In much of the literature it is assumed that somehow there is a common understanding of social change. These authors suggest five goals that are the elements of social change: improvement of the quality of life through the resolution of shared problems; reduction of the level of social inequalities caused by poverty, racism, and sexism; the exercise and preservation of democratic values as part of the process of organizing; enabling people to achieve their potential as individuals; and the creation of a sense of community (p. 10). The difficulty with taking this list of goals as the basis of social change is the mixture of those parts that can be realized locally and those that require state intervention, changes in social policy, or changes in the wider economy and society. Issues like inequality cannot be improved at the local level but groups from the local level can be involved in wider campaigns to create pressure for change. We quickly hit the limits of local work. Communities live the consequences of social inequality. Local organizing has to find strategies to address this question, but at the same time it is necessary to accept the limits of local work and the necessity to be involved in wider struggles and campaigns in order to reach these social change objectives.

## POLITICS OF ORGANIZING

Community organizing faces a contradiction between analysis and practice. On the one hand, we have constructed a strong critical analysis of the inequalities inherent in the social, political, and economic system, including in areas such as class, gender, and race, as well as a critique of the impact of the economy derived from an ecological perspective. On the other hand, our practices are shaped by the need for pragmatic and concrete results. As a consequence, the practice seems to be shaped by theories that are derived from much more moderate frameworks and conventional assumptions. The radical analysis leads one to conclude that society needs to be transformed, while the practice, at best, brings about small, incremental reforms. In other words, radical practitioners have one type of analysis but have difficulty linking it to the following question, which is more difficult: how do we connect a critical analysis with our practice? This is a difficult task, and one that has evades simplistic solutions. The question, however, needs to be confronted, even if the responses are incomplete.

In order to explore these issues, we need theory. Usually when I have these discussions with community organizers in workshops or in the classroom, a glaze rolls over the eyes of students or the audience as they immediately begin to think of their next tasks or their shopping lists or just about anything else. Theoretical discussions are assumed to be abstract, distant from reality, boring, and an unnatural pursuit of academics with too much time on their hands. However, theory needs to be understood more as "(an) attempt to make sense of ... encounters with the world, to look for patterns and regularities in order to predict the outcomes of ... actions ... the overall purpose being to create greater understanding of the world" (Popple, 1995, p. 31). Albert et al. (1986) acknowledge the tensions in the use of social theory. They state:

> social theories cannot help us make testable predictions in the manner of physics and chemistry.... But, nonetheless, we can use powerful social theory to explain relationships; to envision possibilities and delineate trends that may impede or promote those possibilities; and to make "probabilistic predictions" about likely outcomes of current activities. (Albert et al., 1986, p. 5)

Our expectations of theory therefore have to be limited, and recognize that it can be used as a guide rather than a recipe for social change. But theory does not necessarily reside solely in the minds of those who write books and, at times, inaccessible academic articles. Lemert (1993) reminds us that the construction of theory is an everyday practice that is used in order to understand social and power relations. He cites the example of his son, who upon transferring from an alternative school to a traditional one and observing the differences in culture, particularly the discipline of queuing in sex-segregated lines before class, theorized that education was really about social control and discipline. Community organization can draw from traditional theories, but at the same time there can be a process of "common sense" theorizing, which allows us to understand the processes around us and how social intervention can bring about social change. This implies two types of overlapping questions. The first is a perspective that is shaped by examining our underlying values and constructing a basic social standpoint. It tries to set out both an analysis of the society, with an outlook and vision that at times are prescriptive, and the related goals for social transition. The second, which often accompanies the first, is a theory about how change takes place, including a discussion of human agency and related social processes. Thus, we bring two interrelated components—one that helps us shape our social and political vision, and one that contributes to our understanding of what to do to get there.

In order to build a vision of the longer-term direction of organizing, acknowledging underlying values is the first step. Fisher (1994) uses four perspectives. These are the types of underlying values that shape our stance and help us to name the objectives that we are working towards. The first value he calls a reactionary perspective, which is shaped by values that promote efforts to stop social change and to decrease the power of the lower class and minority groups. The second, a conservative perspective, are those values that attempt to maintain the political and social status quo. It is important to keep these two perspectives in the discussion because there is an illusion that organizing is about promoting social justice and progressive social change. Those on the right of the political perspective have used organizing techniques to promote their own agendas such as anti-abortion, opposition to gun control, or the Tea Party campaigns in the USA. Thus, the introduction of "reactionary" and "conservative" into the discussion is an important reminder that the methods of community organizing can and have been used by the right to defend their interests, or to roll back social gains. On the progressive side of the equation, Fisher uses the term "liberal" to describe those who promote more limited social changes that do not actively challenge the existing social and economic system. He uses "radical" to describe those who see the capitalist system as the cause of social problems and see organizing as a way to make more basic changes as well as win concrete gains. Fisher's summary of these political orientations helps us to define our general stance but they do not illuminate the social and political processes that may lead to social change. They are important, however, because they bring out basic social visions.

What are we trying to achieve? If the aims of community organizing are to win limited reforms, then the liberal perspective is the one that shapes its vision. It prioritizes specific outcomes and focuses strategies on making those gains that bring benefits to the community. These might include improved housing conditions or services. Pluralist theory is the underlying theory attached to this viewpoint and it is perhaps the dominant one in community organizing. This theory argues that power in society is not concentrated in a particular group but is diffused between competing interests. There is continual bargaining between groups on a variety of social issues and concerns. The state stands outside of these conflicts, and it plays a role in mediating and resolving disputes and claims from different interest groups. With this perspective, community organizing plays a role "that is acting in supporting and encouraging participation in political and administrative processes" (Popple, 1995, p. 33). Pluralism directs practice to the formation of pressure groups and advocacy for specific social change within the limits of the system.

Fisher's use of the term radical is part of the tradition of the left. The traditional left sought reform through social democratic parties and the electoral process or through revolution—seizing state power. In both cases the working class was the change agent, acting through their unions and political parties. Community organizing has been problematic because the connections between community and class within it are unclear. In the 1960s and 1970s, there was a renewal of left theory. Attempts were made to build from the traditions of social democracy and orthodox Marxism while including new elements.

A traditional left critique began with class power and interests and examined the ways that this power operated in the community. It also examined how the class struggle could be pursed from the community and in alliance with other working-class organizations. Further, the analysis of the role of the state argued that the state represented the interests of the "ruling class," but with contradictions and tensions that permitted social reforms that played a stabilizing role. Within the community movement, a revolutionary socialist vision emerged. Popple (1995) argues that community workers used this analysis to understand the basic inequalities of capitalism and to pursue class struggle at both a local and regional level, but outside of the workplace. Marxism contributed to a radical analysis and vision, despite its limited contribution to discussions of gender and race. It believed that the working class was the main agent of social change; however, beyond building class-based alliances or a revolutionary party, the practices in the community itself stayed within the boundaries of pressure group politics. Local groups pressured for limited gains within the boundaries of the possible.

Getting past this contradiction is perhaps the most important challenge for radicals. Combining a pragmatic practice with a vision of wider social change and a related strategy is the key to moving community organizing from a liberal to a radical perspective. One of the elements that help to move past this paradox is a concentration on the processes of community organizing. The immediate goals become subordinated to the democratic processes and politicizing experiences that come with engagement in social struggles. Thus, if a campaign for better housing exposes participants to the structures of wealth and power, discusses collective options such as cooperatives as alternatives, demands state support for housing, and exposes the limits and inherent problems of a market-based housing strategy, then people may become more politicized through that process. In other words, organizing is an opportunity for political education. Further, creating social solidarity and opportunities for participation produces a network of citizens that can act in their collective interest on other questions and join in campaigns on wider issues. Thus, even though the concrete outcomes of a campaign from a pluralist or radical orientation may be the same, the goals of the latter are longer term and linked to an understanding that ongoing social processes are a necessary precondition for fundamental social change to occur.

The feminist movement has made a significant contribution to shaping the vision and processes of community organizing that goes beyond the limits of class analysis. Popple (1995) argues that feminist currents in community work grew out of two perspectives. The first was a critique of the leadership role taken by men in the field of organizing, particularly in the 1960s. The second recognized that women and their children represent a key constituency for community workers, and that many of the issues and concerns that shaped social struggles flowed from the experiences of women. Therefore, the starting point for community work had to include the experience of women's oppression. Women pointed out the theoretical weaknesses in the traditional left theories through their participation in the growing feminist movement of the 1970s. They argued that the struggles of women needed to be included as a central element in community organizing. For example, in the United States and

Canada, the struggles of welfare mothers for social and economic rights are a vivid example of women taking a leadership role in a social struggle. At the same time there were many tensions with male organizers over this development (Kruzynski and Shragge, 1999).

The feminist perspective modified strategies and visions. It shaped a wider understanding of what constitutes the struggle for social justice. It is a comprehensive approach to social change. This position is argued by Adamson et al. (1988):

> Collective action can reshape our lives and the world around us; it can also change the way we see ourselves—not as individuals struggling in isolation to survive, but as part of a collective of shared interest and vision. This can be a transformative and empowering experience and demonstrates in practice the limits of individualism. Changing society is a way of changing ourselves. (p. 155)

The vision of social equality and the connection between people and political transformation is a key position that forced many organizers to rethink their own values and theories of social change.

Callahan (1997) argues that feminist community organizing includes all of the traditional elements of community development but

> what distinguishes feminist community organizing from other approaches is its insistence that all activities must be informed by an analysis of gender (and race and class) and modified on the basis of this analysis. It is also characterized by its commitment to a social movement and by its attempts to connect local efforts to those taking place in other jurisdictions and at other levels. (p. 183)

The organization's links to a wider movement is a crucial point, and herein lies one key connection to social change. The danger of any community organizing process is to remain isolated at the local level. Building wider connections to movements for social change is a way to support a change agenda and strengthen this connection between local and wider activism.

Popple (1995) discusses anti-racist analysis and practice as another dimension that has important implications for practice. In the United States, the civil rights movement was an impetus for community organizing and social change in Black and other minority communities. The movement had a huge impact on consciousness and energized many different innovations and challenges to the White power structure. In addition, riots and overt rebellion in cities created the conditions that pressured their governments into supporting new social programs that were largely controlled and organized by the Black community and its organizers (Fisher, 1994). In Canada and Great Britain, anti-racist practice reflects changes in immigration, the growth of new immigrant communities, and their subordination in the labour market. The work of the Immigrant Workers Centre presented in the last chapter is an example of practice with this perspective. Resistance to racism had to be integrated into practice and community work had to provide opportunities for different groups to develop their own cultural formation and build autonomous organizations. But, at the same time, both feminism and an anti-racist perspective challenge the role of White male organizers and the position they have held in many organizations. They have pushed the debate further and forced a re-evaluation of the complexities of power. A class-based analysis was not able to get at other forms of oppression. These new forms had to be explicitly acknowledged and the struggles against them legitimated. Further, new and diverse voices had emerged and challenged the wider community movement and sought support from it. Like other aspects of organizing, both feminism and anti-racist perspectives contain elements in common with the radical perspectives and acknowledge the necessity of fundamental social change. At the same time, there are tendencies within these perspectives to share a pluralist theoretical framework that favours increasing participation within the system through pressure group activity, rather than challenging its legitimacy.

Gutierrez and Lewis (1995) integrate a feminist and anti-racist perspective. They argue that the goal of organizing is "the elimination of permanent power hierarchies between all people that can prevent them from realizing their human potential. The goal of feminist organizing is the elimination of sexism, racism, and other forms of oppression through the process of empowerment" (p. 98). They see organizing as a holistic process bridging differences between women based on such factors as "race, class, physical ability, and sexual orientation with the guiding principle that diversity is strength" (p. 98). One of the key elements that comes out of the feminist and anti-racist writing is the necessity of shifting leadership, diversifying who plays these roles in organizations and thus changing the face of both organizers and leaders. Further, the analysis of problems should be from the perspectives of women and minorities if power in community organizations is really to shift. Thus, these perspectives incorporate the connections between race, class, and gender with a process of social inclusion of these groups in the organizing process aimed at basic social change.

All of the above perspectives can be described within the general category of conflict theories. Pluralism examines conflicting group processes within a framework of diffuse power relations, while Marxism, feminism, and anti-racism present an analysis of how power operates in society from the perspectives of class, gender, and race. Clearly, these accounts push community organizing into a conflict mode, challenging the dominant power structure. These are the implicit assumptions of the community action perspective that follows. However, not all approaches to practice share a conflict perspective. The locality or community development model that is discussed below is shaped by consensus-building, which acts to obscure interest and power. There are a variety of social theories that underpin this approach, including general systems theory, which presupposes that all groups in society share common interests and values. The practice that follows can lead to support for the dominant power relations, and it can lead to the creation of community processes that may bring limited improvements to local conditions but not wider social change. As I shall argue below, community organizing can be used as a tool to attempt to change society, or it can play a far more limited role by helping communities adapt to the oppression and the dominant interests of the wider society. Thus, we need to acknowledge theories that shape the latter and dispel the illusion that community organizing is automatically connected with a tradition of radical social change.

By outlining these perspectives, are we any further ahead? The basic paradox of organizing, using a radical perspective, is defined by the differences between how we may analyze society, how we work towards social change, and—related to the latter—how we may define and understand social change. The above perspectives are important for making values and analysis explicit. But with the exception of the pluralist and the Marxist perspectives they do not shed much light on the basic question—what are the processes that can bring about progressive social change? This is an extraordinarily difficult question, particularly if one is grounded in the realities of everyday practice. How does one work from a radical stance in organizing and do something that goes beyond practice shaped by a pluralist, pressure group orientation? For example, there is often confusion between the militant tactics that a group might use that would imply a radical stance and their underlying aims of immediate reform or social inclusion. To accomplish a particular goal such as improving local housing conditions, a group might occupy the offices of a municipal housing inspector as a means of getting inspectors to force landlords to make change. However, the practice is still within the limits of the pluralist assumptions about power. Is community organizing limited by the traditions of creating pressure groups, making demands, and fighting for victories that are only within the boundaries of what the system has to offer? It is, if the only goal is to make gains—that is, to focus on outcomes. This was certainly the dominant model that grew out of the 1960s. However, when organizers moved to the left in the 1970s and also began to incorporate feminism or anti-racist politics into their ideologies, there was a shift in emphasis. The process of organizing became important. The analysis was that organizing for specific gains was important, but at the same time, it was also important that people built an understanding of how the system worked, who held power, and the necessity of building toward longer-term change. The basic way that change could begin to happen was through local people who had learned to act and who also understood the context and the limits imposed by that context. Further, the processes through which this occurred became highly valued. Thus, democratic opportunities and participative forms of decision-making needed to be present. Community organizing created opportunities through which people could have a voice in shaping their organizations and communities. We see the development of these ideas in the 1960s through the actions and ideas of the New Left and the women's movement. The emphasis on process implies that social change is a long-term procedure that involves shifts in ideas, analysis, and the creating of alternative democratic spaces. I will now turn to a discussion of models to examine the links between theory and practice.

Bridging longer-term vision and politics with shorter-term engagement in the struggles for justice in everyday life is a central challenge. The French writer André Gorz (cited in Bond, 2008, p. 5) contributed the concept of "non-reformist reform" as a way to bridge demands for specific gains with a longer-term understanding of the process of social change. He wrote, "To fight for alternative solutions and for structural reforms (that is to say, for intermediate objectives) is not to fight for improvements in the capitalist system; it is rather to break it up, to restrict it, to create counter-powers which, instead of creating a new equilibrium, undermine its very foundations" (cited in Bond, 2008, p. 6). The importance here is the idea of counter-power and the process of challenging the system itself through the activity. Marcuse (2012) brings the discussion to the contemporary period. He describes four approaches to reform. Efficiency reforms are designed to improve the efficiency of what exists. Liberal reforms are aimed at improving aspects of policy that are undesirable. Radical reforms seek redistribution of power and reduction of inequality. Finally, "transformative claims" alter relations of power, propose solutions that go to the root of the problem, advocate redistribution of resources, and prioritize human use over economic value. The demands for transformation are system challenging. However, the reality of an on-the-ground struggle is more complex. Therefore, these demands "may include, in practice, liberal and radical proposals, but argue explicitly that their necessary ultimate goal goes beyond these and must be transformation" (Marcuse, 2012, n.p.). Taking these ideas into the organizing context, Eric Mann (2011) defines transformative organizing as follows:

> Transformative organizing recruits masses of people to fight militantly for immediate concrete demands ... but always as part of a larger strategy to change structural conditions in the world.... Transformative organizing works to transform the system, transform the consciousness of the people being organized, and, in the process transform the consciousness of the organizer. (p. x)

With these perspectives, I present the traditional models of community work and propose an alternative that builds from the "transformative" perspective.

## STRATEGY AND MODELS

Community practices bring two different traditions of social change strategy. The first comes out of a social action tradition and involves exerting pressure on specific targets—governments, corporations, and so forth—in order that these bodies implement some kind of change in policy or behaviour. The impact of these changes would improve people's lives at the local level. The second tradition is the creation of a service, program, or developmental process at the local level that can ameliorate a problem. This is the action-development dichotomy. However, returning to goals raised by Rubin and Rubin, neither of these inherently expands democratic or learning opportunities. Social action work may be carried out by advocacy agencies or professional activists who do not necessarily organize people to participate in these campaigns. Similarly, service provision or development can be controlled by professionals and does not necessarily involve direct participation of people at the local level in the process of organizing and managing these services. In contrast, both the action and developmental approaches can provide opportunities for the democratic involvement of citizens and create democratic structures through which people can shape local processes and organizations. The links between social change and community organization are complex and cannot be understood only by listing the characteristics. Both outcomes and processes have importance. Within practices there are elements of social change activities alongside other elements that reproduce inequalities and hierarchical relations. Examples provided in this chapter and those that follow will illustrate these tensions.

## MODELS OF PRACTICE

It was not until the late 1960s that academics, particularly in schools of social work, expanded the literature on community organizing and development and tried to systematically examine its practice. As Rothman points out in his autobiographical essay (1999a), this attempt reflected innovation in the field and new contestation and mobilization of poor people. During the 1970s, several edited readers were published in the United States to examine the emerging practices. Perhaps the most enduring of these texts was *Strategies of Community Organization: A Book of Readings* (Fox, 1970). This book has gone through many new editions but the core framework remains the same. It is based on an essay by Jack Rothman, "Three Models of Community Organization Practice," published for the first time in 1968. As Rothman (1999a, 1999b) points out, these models were not conceived in abstraction or with clearly delineated theories but were constructed from his observation of the actual practice of his students in that period. The durability of these models reflects some of the continuity in practice; however, they have to be read as a way to pull out similarities in a world of blurred boundaries.

Rothman sets out three distinct models, but acknowledges that in the world of practice they are not mutually exclusive. The three models are locality development, social planning, and social action. There continue to be advantages to this classification of models because they enable the reader to examine the underlying assumptions and social change strategies that are implicit in each. The key elements that can be pulled out of the models include the relationship and analysis of social power, that is, who has it and who doesn't, and the implication of these understandings for the processes involved in organizing. The following is a brief overview of Rothman's models.

The locality development approach is based on assumptions of common interest among groups in the wider society. It assumes that through this common interest social problems can be solved by bringing together representatives of as many groups as possible with each contributing in their own way. Community change can be pursued "through broad participation of a wide spectrum of people at the local community level" (Rothman, 1999a, p. 23). It is a model that includes the diverse interests of the local community and emphasizes social processes. For example, if hunger is the problem, a food bank can be set up through a process of consensus-building among service providers. Conflict is absent from this approach, and it is assumed that common interest overrides differentials of power, income, and wealth at the local level. We will see later how this model has become increasingly important in recent years and how its assumption of common interest acts to maintain the status quo and either directly or indirectly supports ruling relations. At the same time, it is a model that supports direct involvement of citizens and confers responsibility on them for local activity. This is a strength that is inherent in the model but it is the direction of this participation that remains problematic.

The social planning model is a technocratic model that emphasizes a top-down approach to problem solving. It looks for technical solutions, and it believes in rational tools and the expertise of professionals. The planning processes begin with organizations that are often located outside the community, including government bodies, and its intervention is in the form of specific services or programs that are designed to meet particular needs. It may involve residents in the process but does not usually transfer power to them to manage the programs produced. This model has a long history in social welfare dating back to the 1930s when charities tried to coordinate both fundraising and allocation. The approach continues in the work of Centraide/United Way and other planning bodies. This model will not be developed in this book, as I want to concentrate on those approaches that focus their processes at the local level.

Rothman's third model, social action, promotes changes in power relations and direct action from a segment of the community that is without power and resources. This approach gained a following from activists in the 1960s, a period of challenges to social policies and the wider social order. Conflict is central. Interest and power relations are explicit; they are clearly named in this model. The oppressed, the poor, and so on, are to organize themselves with the support of community organizers and challenge those with power. The goal is for them to gain greater resources and a stronger voice. In the 1960s, and 1970s, when these approaches were developed, students, workers, women, and racial and cultural minorities mobilized and demanded a variety of social and economic changes. Direct action was the currency to obtain these demands. An example of this practice is welfare rights organizing, which is discussed later in the next chapter. It is important to remember, however, that groups on the political right have used the same model to protest against changes gained by other forces, such as access to abortion.

In the organization of this book, I will use two categories of community practice. Community development is derived from Rothman's locality development and will be used in contrast to community action or social action. Minkler and Wallerstein (1999) use a similar approach by contrasting what they describe as consensus and conflict approaches. They argue that the community development tradition is derived from a consensus model, while the social action tradition is based primarily on a conflict-based model. As I have argued in an essay co-authored with Bob Fisher (Fisher and Shragge, 2000), there has been a shift away from an action orientation, which was the most prevalent form of practice in the 1960s and 1970s, to a development approach, which has become more significant since the 1980s. One of the key differences of these models is their underlying understanding of power and conflict. The action perspective acknowledges and challenges power, believing that the role of organizing is to help those without power to build a voice that articulates their interests. In contrast, the development approach aims to build social consensus.

Stoecker (2001) links theoretical perspectives with the models of practice. He argues that the development and action models are rooted in two different theories—functionalism and conflict. Functionalism argues that society has a basic equilibrium or balance; that, in maintaining it, people fall into the roles in which they fit; and that any movement is through individual action or personal change. Further, all people in society share a common interest. Thus, poor people need opportunity and cooperation, not power, as a means of moving out of poverty. Conflict theory, he argues, "sees society as divided particularly between corporations and workers, men and women, and whites and people of color" (p. 3). Conflict provides the means of seeking social change. Power is the key issue in this perspective. The action model is concerned with groups building power to contest issues that affect their lives. The development approach, on the other hand, seeks change by building consensus between those with differing interests and power. However, building power does not imply a specific ideology and is not necessarily for the kind of social change that Stoecker implies. Groups like the Christian Coalition or the Tea Party movement have used action organizing to promote a right-wing agency. Models do not imply ideology or specific content.

The importance of models is to pull out the complexities of practice, along with some of the commonalities, and present them in a systematic way. However, practice does not begin with models. Most people toiling in the community begin by being thrown into situations or jobs ("organizing by the seats of their pants," as one organizer described it) and figuring out what they are doing as situations develop. The real problem with this path is that it makes it difficult for practitioners to reflect upon their work and examine the contradictions that emerge. Models can help in that process because they make the underlying assumptions explicit and suggest the actions that can be derived from them. For example, an organizer may be working towards consensus-building and partnership at the local level and then wonder why she/he is having trouble getting the poor people of a community to represent themselves and articulate their demands. Seeking consensus between people with unequal power and interests makes it difficult for disenfranchised groups to have an independent voice. Thus, if the goal is to help a group gain some control over local institutions, then starting with a partnership/consensus model would not be the best strategy.

There are several limitations of model-building. The complexities and overlaps of practice are not easily represented in model-building, and neither is the movement from one type of practice to another over the life of an organization. For example, an effective social action organization can make gains such as revitalizing a deteriorated neighbourhood, and then act to protect its gains by excluding outsiders or institutions deemed as undesirable (NIMBY, or Not in My Back Yard). Similarly, the movement from action to service provision is a common transition. Organizing is used to gain a voice for a group excluded from local politics and processes, but once the group has achieved success and resources, it can be part of a community network of service provision and not take the organizing further. Models, seen from the point of view of practice, do not represent the shifts and the transitions.

Further, models lack a historical dimension that can situate the evolution of organizing activities within particular contexts. The underlying question is this: why do certain approaches predominate in specific periods while they might coexist, be less visible, or play a reduced social and political role in other times? To understand this, an analysis of the social and historical contexts is vital. Here we enter into the complex interaction between the forces of the wider context to shape practice and the power of human agency to override outside pressures. Fisher (1999) describes this tension as follows:

> Certainly issues of human agency—leadership, ideology, daily
> choices regarding strategies and tactics and so forth—all play
> a critical role in the life of any effort, but the larger context

heavily influences what choices are available, what ideology or goals are salient, and what approaches seem appropriate or likely to succeed. By its very nature, history puts the actions and work of individuals into a larger framework, interweaving the local with the more global, the particular with the broader trends, events, and developments in society. (p. 344)

The context can include a variety of factors such as the balance of social forces—the strength of contesting groups in the society, such as the working class through its unions or other social movements. Another factor is the strategies of the state and the types of programs that follow from its orientation. Further, the wider political and social alignments play an important role in shaping the possibilities for community organizations. Organizers intervene in these wider forces, using their creativity and energy but within many pre-arranged choices, often defined by the resources available for the organizing activities. This in turn shapes the choices for an organization whose survival may be contingent upon a limited range of possibilities that are shaped by state programs and policies. At the same time, the power and forces mobilized from below can limit and shape state policies. It is difficult for these forces to be represented in models, but the models themselves can be situated historically—when they developed, how they developed, and what forces shaped their role and their degree of success.

Sites, Chaskin, and Parks (2007) have examined changing models of community organization within the contexts of wider social transformations, specifically the changes from Fordism and welfare state expansion to the neo-liberal order and welfare state dismantlement. Starting with the models described by Rothman, the authors look at the changes linked to wider societal shifts. The social planning model becomes a model for the provision of "flexible services" in which community-based non-profit organizations along with private funders become more prominent in service provision. The development model becomes oriented towards economic development and comprehensive community initiatives. Finally, the action model moves from grassroots organizing to advocacy and coalition-building as a means to secure support for their activities and to lobby for specific reform. When I present the historical changes in community practice in Quebec, I will come back to these changes and illustrate similar transitions in practice models and orientation.

Another difficulty with models is that they do not make the basic vision of social change explicit. Can, for example, the locality development model used by Rothman be considered as part of an approach that promotes basic radical change—and if so, then how? There is a tendency to identify the social action model or community action as the only model that contributes to progressive social change. The underlying reason for this is the conflictual stance of this model and its explicit critique of social and political power. It is viewed as a means of pressuring those with power for specific concessions. But the practice itself is far more complex and, as I stated above, can be used by those on both the political right and left. There is a fundamental question that needs to be asked of the above models. What are the underlying connections between the practices themselves and the processes of social change? Are there theories and traditions of social change that are implicit in different models of practice? Further, what do we understand about the process of social change and how are these processes linked to practice? In order to find the answer, an intersection between social analysis and politics should be linked to models.

Most organizing and community work is framed by a belief in "pragmatic reformism," that is, improving social conditions within the boundaries of what exists. How can community organizing move beyond this and contribute to basic social change? The issue is complex and it is not easy to separate what are limited gains from longer-term social change because engagement in the "real world" inevitably leads to pushing for specific gains or victories. The key differences between those practices that are limited to specific gains only and those that see practice as part of a process of wider social change is linked to factors such as intention, vision, processes, and alliances, which move organizing beyond the local. Without these, both action and development can contribute to social change. As well, each can equally play a role in maintaining the status quo. For example, some forms of service provision or community development may have a much more lasting impact on groups of people in terms of changing their consciousness over the longer term and helping to create the conditions for mobilization for social and political change. At the same time, social action can be limited to specific local gains and not move beyond that.

## TABLE 1.1

|  | INTEGRATION | OVERLAPPING PRACTICES | OPPOSITION |
|---|---|---|---|
| DEVELOPMENT | Service provision and development schemes based on professional leadership and a consensus model | Service provision at the local level | Building alternatives that create new democratic or non-market economics, new practices that are "pre-figurative" |
| ACTION | Pluralist pressure group organizing | Organizing people in a neighbourhood to pressure for local improvements | Social movement organizing and critical consciousness, challenging the legitimacy of existing power relations |

Table 1.1 expresses the relationship between the development and action approaches and the question of social change. I have used the terms "integration" and "opposition" in order to contrast the underlying politics of practice. Integration strategies are used to increase people's participation in the system as it is, or to enlarge resources, or to distribute some goods a little more fairly without challenging the basic assumptions of the system itself. These would be linked to efficiency or liberal reforms or claims, as discussed by Marcuse above. This can happen either through pressure group tactics or through a variety of social programs. For example, local organizing to pressure the municipal government for improved traffic patterns or garbage pickup can improve the quality of life in a neighbourhood, but it does not challenge the car-dominated streets of cities or the patterns of waste production. Similarly, programs such as job readiness attempt to place people in the labour market but do not necessarily raise questions about working conditions, or about the pattern of linking jobs to participation in consumer culture. Integration involves those practices that support the maintenance of the fundamental power relations of our society and the ideology that justifies these beliefs, as well as those practices that are designed to help people either meet their needs or make gains within the existing structures and processes. It assumes that the system can expand to accommodate and bring people into either the jobs or the lifestyles defined by corporate capitalism. It does not question the limits and the competitive nature of the system. Organizing within

this approach does not go beyond either the limitation of local, winnable demands or service and development.

In contrast, those working on the opposition side understand local organizing as part of a process of fundamental social change. This can include both organizing opposition to different aspects of society, such as policy on forms of oppression and inequality, as well as creating local alternatives such as cooperatives and services. These practices challenge the basic relations of power and create an alternative political and social culture based on democracy and direct control of the citizens of these organizations. These are part of Marcuse's concept of radical reforms or transformative claims, and of transformative organizing as Mann defines it. Further, the process of reaching these ends is achieved through mobilizing citizens to play an active role in these changes. This is a key element and the one aspect of practice that has been reduced since the 1980s. Power relations can be challenged and shifted only through collective actions. Community organizing, to be a force for social change, has to be able to mobilize locally but in conjunction with wider alliances that share a politics of opposition.

The differences between these perspectives are not always clear-cut and it is harder to classify actual day-to-day practices. It is for this reason that I have added the middle column—overlapping practices—to the table. In some respects, the actual activities are less important than the processes around them. This means, for example, that specific demands, campaigns, or services at the local level may fall within a process of building opposition. The process of organizing is key, not just the outcome. It includes raising a critical consciousness for those participating in the organizing process and linking the specific demand, campaign, or service to the necessity of social transformation as the means to achieve social justice and democracy. In addition, local work is linked to broader social movements and coalitions that are part of a struggle for social change.

Table 1.1 illustrates the dimensions of integration/opposition along with the action/development approaches. In the chapters that follow, I will provide examples that fall into each of the quadrants.

Integration/Development is currently the dominant practice approach in the wider community. The practice approach includes community development, which will be defined in more detail later, but its characteristics include social partnerships, supporting civil society organizations, and consensus-oriented strategies such as asset-building. Change is understood as an internally defined, local process and solutions to social and economic problems are sought within what already exists in the community, although outside resources may be required. Local democracy through participation of citizens is a factor, but the focus is limited to local improvement with an underlying assumption that self-help is a primary element.

The quadrant labelled Integration/Action is primarily a pressure group approach, which assumes political pluralism in the wider society. The goal of the organizing in this area is to gain local improvements by applying pressure on those with the authority of power to bring about those changes. This approach also focuses on the local, with some alliances with others who have a common interest. Some of the organizations have a longer view of building power but this is within the boundaries of local improvement. There is often confusion between "radical" or disruptive tactics and the more traditional goals that these tactics are used to reach. In both of the Integrative quadrants, there are elements of the practices that contribute to wider social change, but this is not their primary focus. It is an unintended consequence of people working together for social improvement and beginning to build solidarity and a critical analysis. It is this blurring that creates the overlapping categories shown in Table 1.1.

Both quadrants under opposition contain practices and organizations that advance wider processes of social change. Their orientation goes beyond immediate goals and specific practices that are shared, at times, with those of an integrative orientation. This does not happen by accident, but through a self-conscious commitment to these processes that includes intention and vision. Intention implies understanding what the practice is trying to do and naming it. In his book arguing for eco-socialism, Kovel (2002) writes that intentional communities and intentionality can be understood as material forces. He continues, "the generation of some kind of collective 'intentions' that can withstand the power of capital's force field will be necessary for creating an eco-socialist society" (p. 194). Naming the essence of our work is the key aspect. There are risks involved in this. What will the implications be for the sources of support? Will it upset "partners"? There is a difficult line between pragmatism shaped by the demands of others and an understanding of the goals of social change. In order to label intentions, there must be an adequate number of people working together who share these directions. It is of little value having intentions shared by a small group of conspirators within the staff of an organization. Community organizations can contribute to the building of a wider oppositional culture. In order for that to happen, the analysis and alternative direction has to be articulated. This leads to the second component—vision.

Vision is naming the long-term objectives of the organizing process and how they connect to the type of society we would like. It incorporates the core values of the organization and relates these to its longer-term goals and directions, as well as the strategies of how to get there. The importance of the vision is that it orients the politics of the organization and helps sustains the direction over time. Gindin (2002) expresses an example of vision in the context of the resistance to corporate globalization.

> Social justice demands reviving the determination to dream. It is not just that dreaming is essential for maintaining any resistance, but because today, if we do not think big—as big as the globalizers themselves think—we will not even win small. (p. 2)

This level of vision implies that the community movement has to see itself in fundamental opposition to the basic relations of power and domination in our society, and look towards the alternatives in which all forms of hierarchy and domination are ended. This is a monumental task and it is only in alliance with others that there is even a remote possibility of success. More importantly, without a vision of what is basic, how this connects to what is shorter term, and the related processes, it is impossible to get beyond the day-to-day demands of service or limited campaigns. This does not mean that the vision has to be rigid but it should act to orient practice to both goals and processes. Day-to-day local work requires pragmatic engagement with the pressures of funders and the working for specific objectives. These can lead to the organization having its longer-term goals obscured by the demands of everyday practice. One reason for maintaining and articulating vision is to balance the specific short-term demands with the longer-term values and social change objectives. Differentiating between mandate and vision permits a naming of the longer- and shorter-term aspects of the organization. Specific mandates should be shaped by the wider vision. In other words, it is important that organizations do not restrict their definition of vision to their particular activities. One way of doing this is to emphasize processes and alliances.

The Opposition/Action quadrant comprises those social action organizations that intentionally work beyond the local. Activists from social movements founded many community organizations. For example, the student left of the 1960s and 1970s was involved in establishing welfare rights and grassroots neighbourhood organizations. These organizations mobilized people, contested policies of government, and demanded social rights for the poor. Similarly, the women's movement put in place new services that recognized needs and redefined social issues. Many of the organizations that were established continue to exist and, although they have become less politically engaged, they are nonetheless present in social struggles. Social movements, by definition, have a short life. They rise into prominence and then decline. The organizations put in place by movement activists act as a type of continuity despite the transformations they go through—for example, developing services, with professionals displacing the role of activists and representing those they serve rather mobilizing them. But the initial values and visions do not entirely disappear. In addition, the organizations themselves provide stability and continuity that is absent in most social movements. As new movements arise or campaigns are launched, community-based organizations play a role in supporting and nourishing them and can be a place from which to mobilize and carry out political education.

The last quadrant, Opposition/Development, links services and/or development to processes of social change. The underlying idea is to create alternatives to the present system that can act either as places that are free from hierarchies or as models of an alternative type of society. The organizations with this orientation are democratic and participate in a wider culture of opposition. For example, service organizations that grew out of social movements maintain a commitment to social change work. There is another tradition that falls within this quadrant. It is linked to the creation of economic and developmental alternatives. The economic alternatives remove the production of goods and services from the market and prioritize need rather than profit as the reason for production.

As well, ownership is collective rather than individual. The creation of "green alternatives" such as Eco-Initiatives is part of this orientation. Morrison's (1995) vision of "ecological democracy" requires the growth of democratic and community-based alternatives. These encompass both human services and other activities. He argues that these associations are "the basic venue for moving power away from state and corporate bureaucracies" (p. 139). The creation of alternatives has to move beyond local work and build federated structures that develop "associative democracy" to transfer power from government and market to community. Similarly, Kovel (2002) sees local associations as

> the prefigurative praxes that are to overcome capital in an ecosocialist way [that] are at once remote and exactly at hand. They are remote insofar as the entire regime of capital stands in the way of their realization; and they are at hand insofar as the movement toward the future exists embedded in every point of social organism where a need arises. (p. 217)

Perhaps Kovel overstates the case, but the tradition of creating social alternatives to either the state or capital is a long one, rooted particularly in anarchist traditions. These organizations play several roles including demonstrating that people without managers can create forms of local production and services.

Both action and development organizations committed to social change have an impact on the daily lives of citizens that encourages their participation in social change activities. These processes have the potential to help community organizations move beyond their specific goals and day-to-day activities and create a culture of opposition. Community organizations, particularly those founded since the 1960s, grew out of a tradition of direct and/or participatory democracy. This has created places in which citizens can have a role in shaping their own lives and local communities. As power in our society becomes increasingly remote, instances that are controlled by citizens are increasingly important because they allow for open discussion and debate, and for people to participate in decision-making processes and have a voice on wider issues. Democratic traditions encourage active participation and citizenship and thus reduce the passivity generated by consumer society in which the only real decision people are asked to make is which brand-name product meets their manipulated desires and wants. Real politics is neither about consumerism nor electoral choices every four or five years but about active participation in a society where citizens can represent their own interests and create alternatives. Community organizations offer this opportunity.

# CHAPTER TWO

# GETTING FROM THERE TO HERE: HISTORICAL DEVELOPMENT OF COMMUNITY WORK

People have always organized themselves, whether for mutual aid or to raise their voices for social justice. While the focus of the material in this and subsequent chapters will begin with the 1960s, there are many examples and forms of community organizing and development prior to that time period. The main expressions were through charities, which were run by religious or secular institutions; however, there were many other forms of expression as well. For example, in the early twentieth century, workers in urban areas began to organize to improve their working conditions and, prior to extensive state social programs, mutual aid groups countered the paternalism of charities. Dorothy Williams's (1997) historical research on the Black community in Montreal provides an excellent example.

Black people arrived in Canada as early as 1606 when Mathieu de Costa accompanied Champlain and acted as his interpreter. The Black community in Montreal dates back to slavery, with a small group arriving after the war of 1812. However, local organizations promoting and supporting the Black community date back to the beginning of the twentieth century. The pattern of these activities followed that of other communities during the period of Fordist industrialization. Organizations that contested social and economic conditions were for the most part labour-based and local communities saw the growth of both secular and church-based self-help and mutual aid organizations. The major positions of employment for Blacks at the beginning of the twentieth century were as porters on both the Canadian National and Canadian Pacific Railways. They lived in close proximity to Montreal's central railway stations in the district called St. Antoine. Women were able to find employment as domestic workers. The first community organization to be set up was the Coloured Women's Club of Montreal in 1902, which was established by wives of porters as a reaction to White-only women's organizations. The club provided services that addressed problems of housing, food, and clothing. The community's main church, the Union Congregational Church, was founded in 1907. It was later renamed the Union United Church and it remains a central institution in the Montreal Black community today. It was at the centre of the community's life, providing services and assistance to families and challenging discrimination and racism.

By the end of the First World War, the number of Blacks in Montreal had increased. As part of an international movement of Black nationalism led by Marcus Garvey, the United Negro Improvement Association was established in Montreal in 1919. Rather than promoting integration into White society, it argued both for segregated communities and a return to Africa. This association had an ideology of self-help and community development. The central debate in the era was between those who supported this position and argued that the central social conflict was race; and others who believed that class was the central conflict. There were also those who believed that class and race were equal parts of the conflict; these groups were largely organized by railway workers. Unionization was a complicated question because the unions that organized White workers did not allow Blacks to join. Initially, all-Black organizations were set up—for example, the Order of Sleeping Car Porters in 1918 for those who worked for Canadian National Railway, which became affiliated with the Canadian Brotherhood of Railway Employees in 1921. The Porters Mutual Benefit Association was established in 1917 as a response to the anti-union climate of the Canadian Pacific Railway. The employer supported this mutual-aid organization, which became a centre for Black workers, but it did not have any power to negotiate with the employer. These examples reflect the emergence of collective action along the lines of trade unions and mutual aid for workers. These traditions are present in many communities and are particularly strong in immigrant communities who had to fight both injustice and exclusion from the mainstream, as well as the paternalism of charitable institutions.

The discussion that follows will illustrate the ideas and strategies over the past fifty years and the changes that took place in that period. I will draw on examples from Quebec because it is the place in which I have the most direct experience; however, the situation in Quebec has not been unique. The trends in practice have been shared in the rest of Canada and in the United States. For example, Hasson and Ley (1994) in their case studies of neighbourhood organizing in Vancouver and Jerusalem argue that organizing has gone through several stages. The urban protest movements of the 1960s and 1970s displaced the paternalism that was associated with political machines and/or charity. The period that followed emphasized the partnership or co-production between community and government. Mayer (2009) details three periods for urban social movements. She uses the category of urban social movements—a category which includes community-based organizations—and examines it over several periods as a way of analyzing the historical development of these organizations in Quebec. The first period Mayer discusses is the 1960s, in which there was a shift from factory to neighbourhood as a locus of organizing with a focus on the "reproductive sphere" or "collective consumption." The context of this period was dominated by assumptions of state provision and intervention through a variety of social programs. Demands from community organizations targeted governments at all levels for reforms that would ameliorate poverty and deteriorating inner-city conditions. Organizing was about making demands and putting pressure on political representatives.

The second period, the 1980s, saw a shift in community organizing as the politics of austerity prevailed. In this period, conservatives took over national leadership—notably Reagan, Thatcher, and Mulroney—and aggressively attacked union power and rolled back the social gains of the welfare state in the name of economic responsibility. In this period, with the growth of poverty and unemployment and the restructuring and cutting of state services, urban movements became transformed and concentrated their energies on innovative services and cooperation, a transition "from protest to programs" (Mayer, 2009). In this context, urban protest did not completely disappear as much as new organizations formed that were rooted in local, professionalized services. The legacy of this period is the professionalization and service provision that came to shape much of community work.

The final period corresponds roughly to the end of 1990s. In this period, one of the most important elements was the intensification of neo-liberalism, with governments deregulating international economic exchange and providing less internal regulation for the private sector. Along with this, three other important factors become prominent: the growth of immigration, particularly in urban areas; the transformation of cities themselves; and the impact of the anti-globalization movement. First, the growth of migration increased the number of urban poor and poor people of colour, resulting in a huge labour pool of low-skilled and precarious work. Within these changes, new movements and organizing began through anti-neo-liberal and global justice movements that worked alongside of deprived and excluded groups to fight against the injustices and inequalities in contemporary cities (Mayer, 2009).

This attempt at periodization is not entirely successful; there are continuities and overlaps in the practices between the periods, but differences in the types of practice that prevailed in each particular time. Illustrations will be provided for each period. In addition, elements of the wider context that shaped but did not determine the community practices will be elaborated upon. The key relationship that will be discussed in each section is that between the state, the community, and the sources of opposition in that period. The opportunities and limits of community action become structured in these interrelationships.

## PHASE 1: 1960S TO LATE 1970S—CONFRONTING POWER

The context of the period from 1960 to the mid-1970s was shaped by the growth of the welfare state and greater state regulation on a variety of fronts. In addition, the governments at all levels played an active role in shaping economic development to minimize unemployment and actively support economic growth through state ownership of infrastructure. This is often referred to as the Keynesian Welfare State (KWS). The change in the role of government at the federal and provincial levels began during the 1940s and 1950s but accelerated in the 1960s with the introduction and reform of many social programs, such as the establishment of universal health services and improved benefits for the unemployed. Programs that regulated the minimum conditions for work were improved. With low levels of unemployment and the strength of the trade union movement, particularly in the public sector, there was a generalized improvement of wages and living standards. The period of affluence and growth benefited the working class and these gains were protected and expanded. Poverty did not disappear, but became hidden in this exceptional (for capitalism) period of growth. As the state took over greater social responsibility and provided services and programs, older charities and community-based organizations had to redefine their roles, particularly in relation to urban poverty.

The 1960s acted as a time of renewal for organizing. A spirit of social optimism characterized this period. Basic change seemed possible. Two organizing traditions emerged in this period: one was to make demands on government for change and the other was to create new democratic alternatives, often linked to the provision of a service. These two traditions roughly paralleled the action-development divide, but—as we will see later on—both the politics of opposition and those of integration cross these divisions. In the 1960s and 1970s, the politics of both action and development intersected as part of a wider movement for social transformation.

The following example illustrates an action approach. During this period, there was an increase in low-income people organizing themselves into groups where they found a collective voice on a variety of social issues and challenged the dominant social order, particularly the service and welfare organizations that attempted to simultaneously provide benefits and act to control their behaviour (Doucet and Favreau, 1991; Favreau, 1989; Panet-Raymond and Mayer, 1997). I will present one organization in some detail as an illustration of the practice of this period. The research for this was carried out with Anna Kruzynski.

The Greater Montreal Anti-Poverty Coordinating Committee (GMAPCC)[1] was a coalition of local English-speaking citizens' groups

---

1 This section is part of an article written by Anna Kruzynski and Eric Shragge (1999). The information about GMAPCC comes from several sources. Documents have been gathered through a community/popular archives project in Pointe St. Charles in Montreal, and interviews with activists were carried out during the years 1993 to 1999 as assignments in courses at the School of Social Work at McGill University.

composed of the city's poor—mainly welfare recipients. Citizens from five welfare rights committees, along with two-full time organizers, participated in the founding of the organization in the spring of 1970 (Benello, 1972). GMAPCC's initial mandate was one of community organizing around welfare rights and advocacy:

> [GMAPCC taught] people the power of group participation through successful actions against the welfare office. It [created] a strong body of informed welfare recipients who [were] in a position to demand changes from the government over the laws which concerned their lives. (PERM, 1971)

By 1972, GMAPCC had adopted a statement of principles that covered a broad range of topics: jobs and income, housing and urban renewal, education, justice, consumer protection, mass media, democracy, women, racism, the elderly, workers and unions, language and nationalism, and big business (GMAPCC, 1972). These positions advocated redistribution of wealth and strong government action to reach these objectives.

GMAPCC's mandate was carried out in a number of ways. First, it used confrontational tactics towards winnable objectives:

> GMAPCC and the groups relating to it have focussed heavily on conflict situations and on high visibility confrontations, where pressure is brought to bear on the government at various levels. It creates a clear enemy, and focuses discontent; the motive power is rage and the structural aspect of Oppression is minimised in favour of personifying the enemy—a mayor, a corporation president, a slumlord. (Benello, 1972, p. 476)

Thus, GMAPCC used disruptive tactics such as occupations, sit-ins, and demonstrations in front of welfare offices and other institutions (Shragge, 1994). It also used individual advocacy as a way of ensuring that individuals' rights were protected from the abusive ways of the welfare institution. Advocates, citizens who were trained in the rules of the law, would accompany welfare recipients to the welfare office to plead for social assistance. One of the main roles of the resource people within GMAPCC was to seek out, politicize, and train local leadership. This was accomplished in a variety of ways. First, GMAPCC organized "kitchen meetings" where interested citizens from a particular neighbourhood would come together with the resource people to discuss issues of concern to poor people in their area. The goal of these meetings was to get citizens to participate in GMAPCC actions and to eventually form their own local citizens' groups. Second, GMAPCC members organized regular workshops on a variety of topics for local organizers, for members present at general meetings, and for member groups at their request. Workshops were developed to give the participants the tools with which to organize and build groups; topics included dos and don'ts of organizing, negotiating, block organizing, press, tactics, and power structures.

The first action that GMAPCC organised, in July 1970, centred on the right to have an advocate present when pleading for social assistance. The GMAPCC spokesman explained why the group was demonstrating:

"Many people have a hard time speaking for themselves when they apply for welfare—they're too intimidated ... Our members have studied the rules and they can help an applicant as well or better than any lawyer." (Cited in Radwanski, 1970, July 7)

A series of successful actions followed. For example, the "needy-mother sit-in" resulted in the granting of all their demands: "decentralisation of welfare operations, parity rates for all welfare recipients, and availability of immediate assistance for emergency cases" (Arnopoulos, 1970, July 16). In January 1971, GMAPCC staged a successful demonstration in front of a slumlord's house demanding adequate repairs and restoration of heat in apartments of citizens of Pointe St. Charles (PERM, 1971). In one action, twenty-two people were arrested at a sit-in at the Atwater welfare office. Activists were demonstrating against racism, late cheques, and the poor treatment of women. GMAPCC was quick to follow this with one of its largest actions—the "St-Denis sit-in," which initiated a series of meetings with Minister of Social Affairs Claude Castonguay (Benello, 1972). A series of publications entitled "Welfare means hunger and slavery" was produced for this action, providing rationale and evidence of feasibility for the group's demands. Their demands were increases to welfare rates, removal of policy that limited the benefits of single "employable" young adults, and installation of hospitality booths in all welfare offices. Once again, GMAPCC managed to win its demands:

> Claude Castonguay told a group of anti-poverty workers that ... a general increase in the [welfare] payments is expected ... starting in the fall, a few offices will begin issuing welfare cheques every 14 days to make budgeting easier for the recipients ... He also agreed with the groups' demands for hospitality booths in Montreal welfare offices because they had proven to be useful in provincial offices. (Ferrante, 1972, February 8)

Finally, in 1973, GMAPCC launched a successful campaign to stop Bell Canada's proposal to increase pay phone rates from ten to twenty-five cents.

GMAPCC enjoyed many victories around welfare rights and had a significant impact on the people who participated in its development. Thus, through their involvement in GMAPCC, welfare recipients had a direct impact on government policy and practices. The lessons are important. The poor were not "given" rights but they claimed them. Organizations like GMAPCC argued that reform from above was not acceptable unless the poor and others who are affected by change were to have a voice in these processes. This period marked the beginning of the principle of participation by many groups in social policy development and implementation. But it is important to remember that this voice was won through organizing and struggle. If the struggle is forgotten, and there is not an active participation, then the voices become weakened. Tokenism then becomes the result of representation without organization. Thus, effective representation implies active engagement by the poor people themselves. GMAPCC is an example of the recasting of protest movements in that period as it played a role in the struggle for improved conditions for welfare recipients. It was not solely responsible for the gains made in that period, but it was part of a wider social movement that was pushing for social change in a time of economic expansion and social reform. GMAPCC is an example of a direct action organizing. It was a place for poor people to organize themselves, redefine their lives, build consciousness, practise democracy, and take action. There were many similar movements in Canada and the United States during that same period.

The following is an example of a service organization that embodied similar values and orientations as those involved in social action, and that in fact supported their efforts—the Pointe St. Charles Community Clinic. This was one of a number of clinics established in several working-class neighbourhoods in Montreal (Shragge, 1990). This community clinic, founded in 1968, pioneered a new approach to health care. It is important to remember that when the clinic was established, there was no public health insurance. Patients paid doctors directly and privately or, if one could not pay, charity clinics were the alternative. In other words, health care was not a right. The clinic was organized in order to provide access to health care services in low-income working-class communities. In this context, a coalition of medical students and young doctors and nurses, influenced by the radical politics of the period, joined community organizers and local residents to establish the clinic. They had a wider vision of health care than the traditional medical-illness model. They believed that ill health was connected to poverty and the related housing, working, and general living conditions. Their beliefs led them to a practice that incorporated a variety of strategies, ranging from direct medical consultation to collective actions, often in alliance with other local organizations. Their approach to health care moved from the diagnosis and cure of individual illness to a social analysis with social change as the cure. In addition, they challenged the monopoly of professionals over the definition and delivery of health care. Residents of the community were trained as community health workers, and an active democratic process resulted in professional accountability and not their domination. This community clinic continues to exist. It has grown in size and provides similar services to those provided by the network of government community clinics across the province. However, unlike the others it is not a government agency; it is a community organization with an assembly of local residents as the supreme decision-making body. Although it has become more bureaucratic with its growth and increasingly large mandate of providing a wide range of health and social services, it still has been able to support and lead a variety of community action projects and social struggles. I have included this example to demonstrate that service provision can maintain a social change agenda. This was more common in the

1960s and 1970s, when the political and social environment supported links between service and other forms of action. These two tendencies—social action and service—continue in the community movement. One is to demand changes in policy from the government either as an advocate for different social groups or through the mobilization of those groups themselves. The other is to build local organizations that can provide a range of democratically controlled health and social services.

The political and social context in the 1960s and the 1970s, both indirectly and in some very direct ways, encouraged this movement. The federal and provincial governments enlarged the welfare state, and in Quebec the institutions of a modern state were put in place. Money was available from both the federal and the provincial governments to support social innovation. Funding was provided through grants either to encourage employment for the young (Opportunities for Youth) or to create short-term jobs during periods of high unemployment (Local Initiative Programs) (Keck and Fulks, 1997). Other funding, available from many government departments, supported new approaches in the social and health services. One of the main characteristics of the community movement was its autonomy. The funding did not directly undermine the autonomy of the organizations, and in some cases its withdrawal provoked confrontations with angry members of community organizations. Whether new services were established or protests and pressure groups were formed, the autonomy of the groups from the state was strongly guarded. It was also ensured that the structure of the organizations, their vision, and their activities were not directly shaped by funding.

The period from the 1960s to 1970s provided an opening for social experimentation. A stable and growing economy and a corresponding strengthening and expansion of the trade union movement shaped these possibilities. The challenges issued by both the trade unions and the community went beyond the ideologies of capitalism and promoted fundamental change based on a socialist vision. Further, the movement brought with it demands for a democratization of social institutions. The experiments in the community created an experience of direct democracy that demonstrated people's capacity to manage their own lives and institutions.

## PHASE 2: THE 1980S—MOVING AWAY, MOVING TOWARDS?

The period during the 1980s was one of transition between the tough-minded politicization of the previous period and the redefined role of the community sector within the global capitalism of the 1990s. In order to understand this transition we can look at shifts in both state policy and in the community movement itself. In response to changes in the economy—the ending of a long period of economic growth and stability—political leaders sought new solutions. As discussed earlier, a new era dominated by neo-conservative beliefs and policies was brought in. The welfare state and spending in general were cut, the power of workers was attacked, and unemployment was allowed to rise. The community movement and the trade unions responded to these changes with uncertainty and a defensive posture.

At the same time, identity politics and social movements reshaped the community sector. Beginning with the women's movement and followed by groups such as gays and lesbians, the disabled, new immigrants, and people who had survived the psychiatric system, groups created new services and programs that they could shape and control. Examples include rape crisis centres and shelters, which provided services to combat violence against women. Similarly, services for the disabled were not only places of social provision, but they also helped to reshape the way these groups were viewed and treated in the wider society. There was an emphasis on social rights and on the building of new opportunities. Two directions were manifested: demands for political recognition and legitimacy from the government; and the establishment of alternative services that combined participatory practices and new and innovative approaches to service (Lustiger-Thaler and Shragge, 1993).

The rapid expansion of the community sector brought along with it a growing sophistication and professionalism. Shifting from mobilization and political education to service required skilled providers in these organizations. Individuals who had university training and those who learned through their jobs formed a new leadership for service providers in the community movement. This period began a new relationship between the community movement and the state, particularly at the provincial level (Hamel and Léonard, 1980; Panet-Raymond, 1987). Many community initiatives that began as experimental models would become adjuncts to state services. The combination of a decentralization of government services and clear fiscal limits of the state was an important factor that shaped this outcome. The funding of these services was from the provincial government and negotiations took place through "regroupements" or sectoral coalitions, for example, with representation from rape crisis centres, alternative mental health agencies, or coalitions of groups in neighbourhoods. The politics and policies of service were played out through these relations. This does not imply that the activism, mobilization, and direct action associated with the earlier period disappeared, but that these activities and engagements declined relative to the new directions (Panet-Raymond and Mayer, 1997). Divisions deepened between those community organizations that defined their services in an alternative perspective and those that emphasized professionalism and traditional organizational structures (White, 1997). The funding, the service delivery agenda, and the expansion of the fields of community organization decreased the involvement of these groups in political and social struggles. Thus, in the context of an economic downturn and a reduction in support for the welfare state, the community sector grew in size. The emphasis was on service provision, often innovative, with increased professionalism and a more formalized relationship with the state. As a consequence, community organizations lessened their participation in the mobilization of their respective constituencies, substituting representation by professionals. At best, advocacy replaced direct action organizing, and often it did so within the framework of the promotion of services rather than raising demands for social change. The period of the 1980s reshaped community organizing from a process of grassroots contestation to an establishment of innovative and professionalized services, with these new organizations representing the needs and "interests" of their clients.

## PHASE 3: COMMUNITY AS STATE POLICY—WHOSE COMMUNITY?

The economic and policy directions that began in the 1980s intensified along with unemployment and the disappearance of industrial jobs in the older working-class neighbourhoods. As a result, urban poverty grew. Along with the economic decline, all levels of government maintained cost-cutting measures aimed at social programs. Peck and Tickell (2002) describe this transition as the shift from "roll-back to roll-out neo-liberalism." In the first phase, right-wing governments attacked the welfare state and Keynesian forms of economic development. In the roll-out phase the state policy shifted, taking some responsibility for social provision, but doing so through mobilizing the community and private organizations. Kelly and Caputo (2011) summarize the shifts as follows:

> These strategies are, in part, mechanisms that allow the state to set direction, steer activities, and control the process through which public funds are distributed. While the state is steering, however, the community is supposed to row—that is, the community is supposed to do the work that is required to meet local needs (p. 42).

This phase of community as social policy began to shape community practices. The origins of "community as policy" are reactions to the harsh reforms of the right-wing governments of Thatcher, Reagan, and Mulroney with their emphasis on individual competition and the dominant role of the market. They argued for a society of individuals and drastically cut state services. With the election of Blair, Clinton, and Chrétien there was an attempt to redefine a middle ground or "Third Way." These leaders wanted to differentiate themselves from the previous administrations but did not want to return to the older left statist models. The alternative is a new approach that on the one hand maintains the supremacy of the market while on the other hand creating a form of collectivity—but not the state. Community in many different ways becomes the policy direction; that is, a social policy direction in which the state intervenes but does not provide, thus keeping its commitments low and maintaining the "gains" made in opening up markets under the right-wing administrations. Further, the right-wing administrations had polarized society through their policies. In contrast, the Third Way administrations wanted to build a social consensus with the ideals of community and the renewal of communitarian ideas playing a key role in the process. This revised plan did not bring any fundamental changes from the right-wing economic, neo-liberal agendas, but it was a different strategy of obtaining the same ends with less confrontation and a softer rhetoric. Popple and Redmond (2000) discuss the consequences of this shift in the UK, but their analysis also applies in Canada. They state that "the danger for community development has been its adoption as a tool to dissipate and address social disharmony, rather than as a method to assist disadvantaged and oppressed communities to press for increased and more appropriate resources and services" (p. 394).

From 1960 through the 1980s, there was a steady growth in the capacity and the organization of the community sector as more stable relationships were established with the government. The tendency of the previous period to give both responsibility and some forms of assistance to community services has continued to the present day after becoming consolidated and formalized through structured partnerships (Panet-Raymond, 1992). Service delivery that meets with prescribed norms, and that is defined by particular program-related funds, has begun to shape the community-state relation. Conflicts are played out in the processes of negotiation between regional bodies that allocate funds and the various sectoral organizations that bring together the community-based services. These relationships were formalized by 1995 in Quebec with the creation of Secrétariat à l'action communautaire autonome (SACA; the Secretariat of Autonomous Community Action). This body was established as a response to demands from community organizations for recognition and ongoing support for regroupements (coalitions of local or sectoral organizations) and those working to defend social rights. In addition, a consultative committee was appointed with representation from community organizations. A policy on recognition was adopted in 2001, including a definition of autonomous community groups and characteristics such as citizen involvement and a mission of social transformation (Lavoie, Panet-Raymond, et al., 2011). As with many relationships between community organizations and the government, this one embodies tensions. On the gain side, many organizations, including those defending social rights, have received funds and are financially more stable. On the other side, most groups have ended up in subcontracting relationships with different ministries to provide specific services.

At the same time, opposition was expressed less through direct mobilization of citizens and direct action but more through coalitions, particularly those opposing major changes in unemployment benefits or social aid. There were several large and significant mobilizations in this period that demanded poverty reduction policies. Two international marches were mobilized by the women's organization Fédération des femmes du Québec. Both the march of 1995 and that of 2000 raised key issues of poverty, particularly as it affected women. Another significant event in this period was the mobilization of le Collectif pour l'élimination de la pauvreté. Their work was impressive, carrying out an extensive education program across Quebec and a petition drive that netted 212,000 signatures. This resulted in a law adopted by the National Assembly in 2002, Bill 112, to eliminate poverty. All parties supported it. For this discussion there are several important points. First, all three of these campaigns demonstrate that making demands and mobilizing support for them did not disappear with the transformation of the community sector. Moreover, the mobilization was built from these organizations. Second, the scale and visibility of the organizing was large, well beyond anything that local groups could manage on their own. Third, the leadership was run by women and their organizations, giving them prominence and importance. However, the outcomes were very limited and in ways the actions, although highly visible and broadly supported, did not confront or challenge the power or authority of government but simply appealed for changes. Poverty continues and increases—and worsens for many. To demand that the government eliminate poverty is at best naive. The outcome of the first women's march resulted in greater recognition and support for the emerging social economy.

New avenues have been pursued by the community sector as a means to counter economic deterioration. Beginning in the mid-1980s, new initiatives became the impetus for the formation of community economic development (CED) organizations (Fontan, 1988, 1994). Government agencies from the municipal through to the federal level have coordinated their allocation of funds and shaped the activities of these agencies. Some of the groups involved have used government workfare programs to organize ways in which those excluded from the job market could find training and at the same time build local networks of social solidarity (Shragge and Deniger, 1997). The newer groups have linked social insertion with socially oriented community businesses (Ninacs, 1997). These new practices have created a space for those marginalized by the economic crisis as well as a way of building cultural and social alternatives, and this in some ways represents the beginnings of a small social economy among the poor. Yet, at the same time, there is a process that has transformed these organizations to become managers of government programs and promoters of local, private economic (capitalist) development (Fontan and Shragge, 1998). This tension is described in the case study of Chic Resto-Pop that follows.

## CHIC RESTO-POP: PRACTICES AND ISSUES[2]

Twelve welfare recipients organized Resto-Pop, a community restaurant, in 1984. They had two purposes: to create jobs for the founding members and others on social assistance, and to provide quality, hot, and inexpensive meals for the poor in the community. These goals have been realized in the intervening years and the organization has both grown and broadened its activities. It has introduced a mobile kitchen to provide meals to local schools, and it puts on day camps in the summer. In addition, a musical festival, which is now part of an autonomous organization, was introduced in 1992. Resto-Pop serves three meals a day, five days a week. In 1984 it served meals for 50 people; in 1990, 250; and by 1995, it had reached 800.

Resto-Pop is a non-profit organization managed by a seven-member board of directors; they come from the church and the professions, and they are almost equally divided between men and women. There is no staff representative on the board, and until recently there was no general assembly. The operating budget for 1994 was $800,000. Slightly less than half of that was from the three levels of government; the rest was raised from meal sales, bingo, and donations. There are nineteen full-time employees under the supervision of the director. Four employees are involved with administrative work, two coordinate the restaurant, and fifteen others carry out the general work.

Job development and training is a central concern of Resto-Pop. It takes in 105 trainees a year on an ongoing basis. The length of training varies between six and fifteen months. The trainees are all receiving welfare and are participating in a workfare program called Expérience de travail (EXTRA). This program was a controversial part of a welfare reform

---

2 This case study is derived from previous work co-authored by Jean-Marc Fontan and Eric Shragge (1996).

introduced in 1988 and many community organizations that could accept trainees have boycotted it. They have criticized the program because it did not create real jobs, claiming that the lack of jobs made whatever training was received useless. Resto-Pop members believed that their use of the program was in the interest of welfare recipients; they felt that it connected those marginalized by poverty to a wider social process in which their labour was the basis of social reintegration. Thus, Resto-Pop has attempted to use the shifting economy and the redefined welfare state to be part of a wider movement in Quebec to create a locally based social economy.

According to one Resto-Pop staff member who supervised the trainees, participants are treated as workers with the responsibilities and rights attached to that role. This is an attempt to break the dependency and passivity associated with individuals who have received Social Aid (welfare) for a long period. The goals of the training are to promote socially useful work that permits the individual to rebuild confidence, improve general work habits, and learn new job-oriented skills. The coordinator of Resto-Pop explained that one of the most important functions of the organization is to support the trainees with their program linked to work preparation. Psychological support and literacy training are provided by a neighbourhood organization. The content of the training goes beyond the immediate tasks necessary for running a community restaurant, and it includes topics such as social rights. The longer-term goal of training, according to one of the founders and a former coordinator of Resto-Pop, is to demonstrate that the marginalized people of the district can be something other than clients of community organizations; they can also be workers and effective managers.

A Resto-Pop self-study reports that the most frequent users of their program are single men, with an average age of forty-five, who live alone and are receiving welfare or employment insurance. They eat, on average, six to eight meals a week at the restaurant. Resto-Pop provides more than meals; it is also a place for socialization where one can meet others in a similar economic situation. The large dining room is also used by community organizations to provide information and discussion about such issues as the social origins of poverty and the rights of those receiving welfare. Thus, Resto-Pop is simultaneously a training program, a socially supportive environment, and a place that provides meals for members of the local community.

In the fall of 1995, Resto-Pop moved in a new direction. The staff person in charge of training raised several critiques about the training and related government policies. He argued that the government continued to think about and apply its welfare system as though it was a system of last resort, acting as if the recipients had invented their own joblessness. Short-term training programs coupled with unemployment had institutionalized instability and excluded many from both economic and meaningful social roles. In light of this analysis, Resto-Pop asked the government to reform its training program and allow participants to stay for three years. The government refused, arguing that they did not want to encourage dependence in a protected environment.

Frustrated by the government's lack of movement in a more progressive direction as well as the continual increase in local poverty, the leaders of Resto-Pop called a conference to examine the underlying economic issues and politics of deficit cutting and the lack of adequate government response. Several hundred participated in this event, culminating in a series of demands and a march to the office of their local provincial representative. Their demands touched on fiscal and monetary policy, minimum wage, job creation, daycare, and training, calling for full employment through a variety of actions and innovations (Chic Resto-Pop, 1995). This event demonstrates the possibility of creating pressure on the government and launching a public debate within the new model of practice that became dominant in the 1990s. Resto-Pop has become both a service and a training centre, whose major goal is to combat the social isolation that is a consequence of poverty while simultaneously finding ways to help those unemployed begin the process of entry into the labour market. Resto-Pop is now part of a wide network of organizations specializing in training and community service. These organizations are called "entreprises d'insertion," which can be roughly translated as "training businesses." There are forty-seven of these types of organizations across Quebec with similar mandates and practices (Collectif des entreprises d'insertion, www.collectif.qc.ca, accessed April 26, 2012). They have received recognition and funding from the Quebec government. This process of receiving support has been a process of strengthening community-based services but also depoliticizing them. The services tend to be innovative and achieve social goals but they do not challenge the underlying issues that sustain and reproduce the social problems they face.

The community practices developed in the 1990s and continuing through to 2012 incorporate the formal partnership arrangements discussed above into the structures of their organizations and their wider relationships. Community organizations are faced with the dilemma of having received greater recognition and funding, which in turn has diminished their autonomy and reinforced their service agenda. With this orientation, groups have shifted from a membership or social-movement base to a client focus. This redefinition is inherently depoliticizing. Clients are to be served and have a less active or non-existent role in either the organization's internal processes or on wider social issues. At best they are represented rather than mobilized. Thus, the dominant form of political representation has become lobbying by coalitions of community organizations promoting the needs of a particular population.

A service orientation brought with it a redefinition of the political, from the earlier period's definition based on direct action and mobilization to the current definition of lobbying and representation. Yet some groups have maintained the earlier traditions of mobilization and direct action. The success of the community mobilization for the recent student strike, or the international mobilization of marches for women, or various campaigns against government cutbacks, have all drawn from community movements. Even though the majority of community organizations are involved in a service or development model, there is still sympathy for direct action. This might not be the dominant element in their practices, but it is still there. We can see that the community movement has indeed changed over the last thirty years. It has moved from an oppositional force to a sector that is highly professional and in many ways is integrated into the state service sector as an important partner, but at the same time there are still traces that remain of the earlier stances and values.

Is it possible to describe the community sector as contributing to the processes of social change? What is the contemporary role of the community sector? Deena White (1997) summarizes its changes as follows:

> The Quebec government, through its efforts to integrate community-level collective action into its social policies, has made considerable headway in transforming radical politics into interest-group politics, grassroots unrest into services by and

for vulnerable social groups, and confrontation into apparent consensus. (p. 81)

This argument can lead to pessimistic conclusions about the possibilities. Other analysts see the situation as having other, greater potential. Panet-Raymond and Mayer (1997) argue that community groups have used a strategy of "critical cooperation or cooperative conflict" (p. 51) in their relationship with the state. They argue that both radical advocacy groups, along with their coalitions, and institutionalized service organizations co-exist in tension. Thus, community organizations are pulled between two poles. The first is that of an oppositional force that raises demands, mobilizes or represents the needs of its constituency, and pushes for some form of social change. The second pole is that of community organizations that have become extensions of the state. Through the process of receiving support from the state, these organizations lose any oppositional character and become partners with the state in the provision of a service. I have deliberately over-polarized the situation, but in order to understand the grey areas we need to understand the poles of the debate.

Looking back, two significant traditions run through the history of the community movement: the direct/social action approach and the development/service approach discussed earlier. One tradition exists as an opposition movement that challenged dominant interests and the wider social order. Its power rests in its capacity to mobilize either large numbers of people or broad-based coalitions into action. The other tradition is one of service development and provision. Over time the community has become more professionalized and service-oriented, resulting in its oppositional role being diminished. New social partnerships between the community sector and the state have become common practice. It is this change that leads me to question the role of the community sector as a vehicle for social justice.

The current conjuncture presents limits, problems, and possibilities. With changes in the economy and the state's reduction of or withdrawal from its commitment to social provision, the community sector has begun to play an enlarged social role. It has taken over responsibilities for various services and entered the chambers of the state to be consulted on policy issues. These might be seen as gains and opportunities, but the consequence has been that the community movement may have lost its critical edge and radical democratic practice. Some argue that the new relationship with the state is "cooperative conflict" (Panet-Raymond and Mayer, 1997, p. 51), but numerous questions remain: what is the source of power that can sustain a conflictual relation with any credibility? What is the power base of community organizations if it cannot mobilize people? How can they defend their autonomy without an active politicized constituency? What happens if the community sector's only source of legitimacy is its capacity to provide inexpensive and innovative services and programs?

The changes implied are contingent upon a professionalized leadership in community organizations. "Professional" does not only include those trained in a university department such as social work, but also individuals who acquire expertise and play a major role in an organization. The problem arises when the expertise becomes a barrier to the participation of citizens. Organizations require staff and people who can provide services within service organizations. The tasks and work of the community sector are far too complex and the work too time-consuming to go down the path of volunteerism. One consequence of this process is that the power of expertise and the power of professionals reduce the control of the organization's wider community. This process contributes to the organization's demobilization, and it gradually results in passivity in which people become transformed into "clients" rather than "citizens" (McKnight, 1995). Equally, there is a danger that the work of the community sector comes to rest on the shoulders of volunteers or self-help. A balance is required in which there is a constructive tension between an active membership/participants and a staff that is accountable to the organization.

The service orientation itself has contributed to a demobilization of citizens. Within this orientation there is a wide variety of practice and forms, ranging from self-help groups like collective kitchens to new community businesses specializing in training, to services for different populations. Many forms of management coexist, from collectives to traditional hierarchical forms. Yet the common purpose is social provision. The tradition of community organizations as a voice of opposition has been shifted. Fewer and fewer groups directly organize and mobilize the poor and the disadvantaged. Rather, for those groups still involved in oppositional activities, they represent populations affected by changes in government policies, sometimes defining their self-interest as service providers as the cause to be defended. Service provision and mobilization are not necessarily in contradiction, but as an organization becomes en-meshed in the demands of provision—and as governments support only the service aspects of their programs—integrating other activities be-comes more difficult. Further, the community sector is not well financed and, for most organizations, there are no long-term guarantees. A rela-tionship of dependency with little equality is thus established, leading to less risk-taking and political engagement.

There are some organizations still engaged in the older traditions of mobilizing and organizing citizens at the local level as a means of op-position. These will be discussed in the next chapter. In the community sector, the opposition comes from coalitions of organizations or "Tables de concertation," which is a form of representation of interest rather that a mobilization of people to represent it. The strength of the community movement, going back to the late 1960s, was found in its capacity to mo-bilize people into action, either to protest and confront governments or to build new forms of local democracy. The danger of the current conjunc-ture is that a professionalized, service-oriented community sector will be legitimized by its competency to serve and represent. At the same time, if it hasn't done so already, it will lose its real source of power—that is to say, organized and active citizens struggling on their own behalves.

# CHAPTER THREE

# THE LEGACY AND TRADITIONS OF SOCIAL ACTION

The legacies of community organizing practice are complex. As I discussed in the previous chapters, neither the development of community organizing nor its action models are necessarily directed at progressive social change. Both have potential if used along with a critical social analysis, a long-term vision, and a strategic understanding of what each can accomplish. In this chapter, I will explore the community action approach by examining several perspectives. I will start with the work of Saul Alinsky, the American community organizer who popularized the method and its strategies. He, more than anyone else, named the process and envisioned the neighbourhood as the place for organizing. All of the organizers who followed learned from him. I will follow this with a discussion of the contribution from the North American New Left. Although their efforts in the late 1960s did not produce lasting outcomes, their ideas and experiments—particularly in new forms of citizen participation and direct democracy—have influenced social and political movements to this day and have shaped experiments in building local alternative practices. The women's movement took the new practices further and added personal dimensions to the political process. A variety of social movements followed that built on these themes and played their own variations. We can see that many radical and social traditions grew out of social movements and community organizing. At the same time, there are many questions and contradictions. The legacy is not always clear and the practices in the community are not necessarily vehicles of social change. The chapter will conclude with several examples of contemporary community action to examine the continuities of this approach.

## ALINSKY AND THE RISE OF SOCIAL ACTION ORGANIZING

Social or community action organizing has a long and almost mythical history. It is the story of building opposition to the dominant social structures, challenging power. It is the story of the oppressed and poor making claims on the rich and powerful. Like any other mythology, the actual history is more complex. When I began my work in community organizing, the biggest name and most famous organizer was Saul Alinsky. He was a pioneer, an innovator—a fast-talking, self-promoting organizer who began his career in the working-class neighbourhoods of ethnic Chicago in the 1940s. Because of his influence, I shall start with his contribution to organizing and then look at the way his approach was reshaped by the New Left of the late 1960s and early 1970s. Then I will examine the contributions of the feminist movement. I have grouped these three together because I will argue that, although each has its own independent legacy, they all contributed important ideas that can be synthesized to bring a broad-based understanding of the processes that link social change and community organizing.

Although there were many examples of pressure group organizing before Alinsky, he was the one who pulled together a systematic practice of community/neighbourhood organizing. He was successful in many projects, was well known both in and outside of the United States, and influenced many organizers that followed. I will not present either his biography or an account of his organizing work, but I will try to pull out some key features, lessons, and debates that have emerged from it. Alinsky was a product of the old left, more social democratic than communist, and carried the traditions of the labour movement. He believed that reform was possible within the structures and processes of capitalism. He promoted a pragmatic approach to social change that emphasized the potential of the poor and powerless to make gains through the processes of community organization. Power is the key element. In addition, this power was built through organization and momentum was achieved by making concrete gains or winning victories. Alinsky (1971) wrote,

> Change comes from power, and power comes from organization. In order to act, people must get together…. The organizer knows that his biggest job is to give the people the feeling that they can do something, that while they may accept that organization means power, they have to experience this idea in action. The organizer's job is to begin to build confidence and hope in the idea of organization and thus in the people themselves: to win limited victories, each of which will build confidence. (pp. 113–14)

The underlying belief was that large numbers of people acting collectively could force changes and make concrete gains.

Alinsky was committed to a pragmatic approach and spoke against an organizer holding an "ideology." On this he wrote,

> What kind of ideology, if any, can an organizer have … he does not have a fixed truth—truth to him is relative and changing; *everything* to him is relative and changing. He is a political relativist … To the extent that he is free from the shackles of dogma, he can respond to the realities of the widely different situations our society presents. In the end he has one conviction—a belief that if the people have the power to act, in the long run they will, most of the time, reach the right decisions. (pp. 10–11)

This aspect has become one of the most contentious issues. Without ideology the methodology can be used for a variety of ends, both left and right, with groups like the Christian Coalition or the Tea Party using techniques of protest learned from the Alinsky tradition to promote a right-wing agenda. Implicitly, Alinsky assumed that change would move in a socially progressive direction to enhance the lives of the poor, the working class, but organization practices without more explicit ideologies tend to be rudderless and can be used to move in many different directions.

Alinsky himself was larger than life and by the 1960s was approximating an urban legend. He was called into many cities to help with the building of organizations in poor communities. Local political establishments often vilified him publicly. The organizations he helped to create were set up to mobilize people, win issues, and make gains. However, the results were more complex than the rhetoric and images. Some of the organizations had relatively short lives—as little as five or six years (Fisher, 1994)—and those that survived beyond that became transformed from being driven by confrontational activists to being led by managers of social and economic programs. For example, one of the better known and more highly acclaimed organizations in Chicago, The Woodlawn Organization (TWO), "became just another business in the community, a nonprofit business almost as removed from many of Woodlawn's problems and needs as the profit oriented businesses"(Fisher, 1994, p. 144).

The legacy of Alinsky is important despite its contradictions. One contribution was that he legitimized and made explicit the role of a community organizer as a form of "professional" activity. He not only described the functions of this work but also believed in the training of organizers, drawing them from the ranks of local leadership. His organization, the Industrial Areas Foundation (IAF), trained many organizers who went on to become leaders in community and social struggles. Another lesson that Alinsky strongly promoted, though it is certainly not unique to him, is that large numbers of people acting through an organization are the source of community power. A "peoples' organization" is the core concept for creating social power. This lesson is self-evident at one level but it is easily forgotten. In recent years in both Canada and the United States, there has been a shift from an emphasis on mobilization of large numbers of people to one on representation of people through coalitions of organizations. The loss of this perspective has in part contributed to a weakening of opposition movements. One can be critical of the form of the organization that Alinsky used, but this basic principle is sound. The creation of popular organizations is the key to building power. In contrast to more generalized protest activity, organizations provide continuity, structure, and a means of sustaining activity.

I will now turn to some criticisms of this approach. However, I realize that it is easy to do this retrospectively. Alinsky promoted a path-breaking method and opened up many new possibilities. We need to see his contribution as being shaped and supported by wider social and political movements, which generated popular interest and a more progressive and optimistic context. His major successes began in the Back of the Yards, an immigrant working-class neighbourhood close to the meat-packing plants in Chicago in the late 1930s and early 1940s, and he found success again in the Woodlawn neighbourhood in Chicago in the 1960s. These neighbourhoods were linked to the social movements of those periods— the anti-fascist and union movement during the earlier period and the struggle for civil rights in the latter (Fisher, 1994). Alinsky's method was to use organization to get those outside of the power structure closer to it in order to negotiate specific concessions. As well, in the periods of his greatest activity, the state played an interventionist role in supporting social development; therefore, it was easier to get support for the organizing and secure victories. Alinsky's pragmatism and mobilization within acceptable boundaries in combination with his confrontational style created a contradictory image of Alinsky organizing—simultaneously radical and liberal.

Turning to criticisms, one can begin with the consequences of his pragmatism. Alinsky and those who have written about him emphasize the necessity of winnable issues as a way of demonstrating the capacity and power of the community organization. What if an issue is not immediately winnable, particularly at the local level—does this imply that it should not be tackled? How does an organization confront fundamental economic and social issues such as welfare, poverty, and so on if the issues that are selected are based on their "winnability" and their potential to contribute to the building of the organization? In practice, change is defined within narrow parameters. This begins to shape the nature of the organization itself. Further, controlled change within pre-existing limits is the outcome, and despite the militant tactics, the actual demands do not pose a threat to basic relations of power and wealth. Organizing becomes channelled into a direction that can be supported by foundations and churches, and one that improves local conditions but remains well within the bounds of small-scale reform that can be organizationally managed and negotiated.

Linked to this problem are the inherent constraints of localism. Neighbourhood organizations that promote local improvement without building alliances that can challenge broader issues remain isolated, and their ability to build opposition is inherently limited. I would describe this as power within. What about power beyond the local, how can this occur? Alinsky recognized this limitation. In his book *Rules for Radicals* (1971), he argued for the use of proxy campaigns as a way to use shares in corporations to confront them and democratize control of large businesses. At the same time, he wanted to broaden his constituency to include the middle class. Neither of these came to fruition. Some campaigns used proxies to enter into annual meetings of corporations and challenge them on a variety of issues, but corporate structures and concentration of ownership mitigated the possibility of small shareholders influencing the direction of those companies. Thus, even with the recognition of the limits of localism, Alinsky and his organizations never really got beyond it.

The idea of training organizers is an important contribution. But the tradition is flawed in some basic ways. Alinsky trained effective organizers in his own tough, "macho" image. These organizers were central to any initiative and provided more than leadership. They helped initiate organizations and played a controlling role in them. However, basic problems and questions can be raised. One is the issue of the power and accountability of the organizer. The organizing process puts the organizer in the centre. The credibility of the organizer rests with his/her ability to recruit leaders and members. The functions of the organizer include building the organization, identifying leaders, and helping leaders to build skills and local visibility. Local issues act as a way to recruit people into the process. In theory, the organizer works him/herself out of a job as leaders build the capacity that is necessary to carry out organizing functions. The realities are more complex. Organizers have a lot of control, particularly in the early stages. As the organization matures, organizers are still there and work closely with leaders to shape agendas and direction. In theory, the role of the organizer is as someone who is able to put forward options and choices for the organization. There is supposed to be an internal democratic process. The problem with this model can be the lack of accountability of the organizer to the leadership and members. In practice the program and approaches to organizing are predefined and participation is a vehicle to sanction the choices already put in place through the initiative of the organizer. I am not arguing that democracy is an easy process, but rather that the organizer has a lot of power in shaping and controlling the process. The organizer role is not clearly defined, meaning that the organizer stands both inside and outside the organization. At the same time, people who become involved in the organization have voted with their feet; in other words, the organizer does not have material power and cannot offer incentives, and those who join do so because of their belief in the organizing process and goals.

A related issue is the characteristics of the organizer himself (I use "him" deliberately here). Alinsky organizing, perhaps inadvertently, is based on the "great man" approach to history. Being an organizer required sacrifice, long hours, and personal charisma. I have presented students with Alinsky's organizing methods via the famous National Film Board and Public Broadcasting films on him, or by having them read his material. The reaction, particularly among female students, is that they cannot possibly become that type of practitioner. An organizer is viewed as larger than life, a dynamic leader. Students feel that this is beyond their reach. The discussion then shifts to the reality of organizing, the day-to-day grind, the multitude of small tasks, the relationship-building processes with citizens at the local level. These are the key elements in effective organizing work. All of these are present in Alinsky's work, but the presentation of his persona overwhelms that reality. The dedication demanded is far beyond what most people are willing to give.

In contrast, Linda Stout (1996) has written a more realistic portrait of an organizer. She describes her transformation from growing up in a poor, southern, White family with little formal education in Appalachia, to becoming an effective community organizer. She acknowledges all of the difficulties, struggles, and self-doubt she met on the way, and the role of supportive relationships in helping her through these difficult changes. Her example is far more encouraging and realistic. Her writing and style was influenced by the changes in politics and ideologies introduced by feminism. The contrast, however, points to the mystique perpetuated among some earlier male organizers that discourages those who do not see themselves as charismatic leaders from becoming involved in community organizing.

Another challenge to Alinsky's approach is on the question of organization and organization-building. His underlying idea was that peoples' organizations are a necessary component of a social change strategy. Here lies the central difficulty, and a major debate in community organization theory and practice: is building an organization the most effective way to promote social change? If not, what are the other options, and if so, what kind of organization should be built? Alinsky believed in forms of organizations that have a formal process and structure. The structures were complex, and they required maintenance and a permanent source of funding. At the same time, the action agenda was more often short-lived and was used to build the structure by recruiting people who had an interest and a stake in working on specific issues. One can question whether maintaining a structure is really worthwhile, given the resources and time necessary to do that, and given that the mobilization is not necessarily enhanced because the organization is in place. Further, the formal structures used by Alinsky and others provide the basis for a shift in orientation from a social action strategy to one providing service or developmental work. Organizations can manage budgets and programs. They also require support to manage their own structures, and they are pushed towards finding the funds to support these structures. For this purpose, they are directed to sources that provide support for more traditional activities, such as service provision. The organization structure has a capacity to manage programs and this indirectly commences a process of demobilization.

I argued another position in an article that I wrote with Glenn Drover in 1979. One of the faults of Alinsky-style organizing was that the process of organizational maintenance took too much energy and too many resources. We put forward a counter position, drawing on the work of Cloward and Piven (1977). A strategy of mobilization rather than organizational building required a small group of "political friends" who could carry out organizing work at the local level. A small group of organizers does not require the same level of resources and can then embark on periodic educational campaigns and mobilization with far less dependence on outside resources. I have come back to this position over the years, as I have seen excellent political campaigns launched at the community level based on direct mobilization of citizens and ad hoc coalitions of organizations. In the next section, we will revisit the organizational question—less from the point of view of the debate on organization versus mobilization and more from the point of view of the direct democratic perspectives emerging from the New Left and the women's movement.

To conclude, the Alinsky approach provides a starting point. It legitimated community action organizing as a vehicle for social change.

It brought the energies of the social movements of Alinsky's time into neighbourhoods and provided another vehicle through which people could make claims for improvements in their lives. In a sense, he took progressive politics and brought them into the community. This was a step forward as previous to that a charity and service model had prevailed. At the same time, there were many limits, debates, and problems, as I have pointed out above. In the discussion that follows, I will examine how the organizers that followed Alinsky borrowed from him, and yet put their own mark on organizing. There is continuity, a layering of approaches, rather than breaks with older forms. We will now turn to the political movements that followed to see how they developed their practice of community organizing.

## COMMUNITY AS SOCIAL CHANGE: THE NEW LEFT AND SOCIAL MOVEMENTS

In many ways the wave of student consciousness and protest of the 1960s shaped my own consciousness, more in terms of stance and attitude than in terms of specific analysis and theory. As I became more involved in community organizing in graduate school and in Montreal afterwards, I met many who were a few years older than I was, and who had been influenced by what can be described as the student movement or the New Left. Many activists graduated from activities in the student movement to struggles in the community. They were armed with an analysis of the wider society, experience in student politics, energy, and dedication, and they found support from government and private foundations. In both Canada and the United States, activists sought new forms of organization and ways to link their analysis to practice. Innovation and a distrust of the "older ways" were present. Many of the experiments did not succeed in the short term, but in the longer term, the practices and values have had an impact. The ideas of the student movement took hold in a variety of activities and social movements that followed, such as the women's, ecology, and peace movements, as well as in neighbourhood organizing projects in Canada and the USA.

In order to understand the innovations of the New Left and the connections between community organizing and social change that were inherent in their politics, I will present a contrast between the New Left and the old left as the starting point for this discussion. One difficulty is that the New Left did not have a coherent ideology and its dominant voices shifted over time. One can talk about the early New Left in both Canada and the United States between the years 1962 and 1968, and the later period from the late 1960s into the 1970s. The former period is ideologically more open; the latter, in many instances, was shaped by a revolutionary Marxist perspective. In the United States after 1968, greater social polarization, violence, and repression led to a New Left that was more taken up by the politics of violence and revolution, was more interested in Third World struggles, and consequently placed less emphasis on the values and experiments of the earlier period. This does not mean that these earlier practices disappeared. In both Canada and the United States many stayed the course and continued to work in communities, building organizations, campaigns, and projects, but these did not share the media spotlight with those organizations that engaged in violent confrontations. However, activists in the later period continued to build on the values and practices of the early New Left. I will focus on this earlier period and examine some of its prominent values, orientations, and practices. These were influential long after the 1960s as they built a foundation for later work in community organizing projects and social movements.

To begin, there were several departures from the older left with the emergence of the new. The old left grew out of several conditions that shaped its politics: the Russian Revolution and the subsequent Cold War politics, the scarcity of the Depression, and the rebuilding after the Second World War. Many in the traditional left, through the parties and organizations they built, believed in reform from above—the potential of economic growth and technology to produce reform and ameliorate social and economic conditions (Breines, 1989). The New Left of the early 1960s did not have much of an affinity for these traditions of the older generation; it was influenced far more by pacifism and anarchism. As Breines (1989) states,

> The vision of the New Left developed in affluence rather than
> depression and fascism, was of a cornucopia of possibilities. A
> social system which provided for everyone, and in which every-
> one participated equally, seemed desirable and possible; class
> was not critical to its vision.... the New Left became interested

> in culture and hegemony: concepts central for understanding
> the hold which advanced capitalism had on people's conscious-
> ness. The old left was preoccupied with "objective conditions"
> of revolution, while the New Left highlighted the importance
> of "subjective conditions." (p. 16)

In addition, the activists of the New Left were based, at least initially,
in the university. They were a generation who lived in a combination of
economic stability and alienation. Universities were in the process
of rapid growth and students critiqued their educational experience as
one that served the new corporate elite. New ideas grew out of these
experiences.

One of the most influential intellectuals of the period was the sociol-
ogist C. Wright Mills. His analysis, departing from the orthodoxy of
the old left, contributed to the ideas that shaped the New Left's analysis
and actions. Central in his writings were the links of the personal to the
political, and the notion of a radical democracy shaped by face-to-face
decision-making. These ideas were developed in the years that followed
and became central to the differences between the old and new lefts. The
belief in the direct participation of people in decisions that affected them
was to have an enormous impact on the approaches to community organizing that followed (Miller, 1987).

In addition, the processes of democracy involved the creation of community for those who shared in a common cause. The key concept was
"prefiguration." Breines (1989) defines the concept as follows:

> The effort to build community, to create and prefigure in lived
> action and behavior the desired society, the emphasis on means
> and not ends, the spontaneous utopian experiments that devel-
> oped in the midst of action while working toward the ultimate
> goal of a free and democratic society, were among the most im-
> portant contributions of the movements of the 1960s. (p. xiv)

Two directions followed in community organizing. The first was not
dissimilar to Alinsky, and focused on power and social issues. However,
this was framed within the belief that organizing had to involve a radical
democratic process based on face-to-face relations. Richard Flacks, one

of the leaders of Students for a Democratic Society (SDS), argued in 1965 that there was a tension between the two types of goals, one involving "a redistribution of wealth and power" and the other being "an attempt to achieve 'community,' to reach levels of intimacy and directness with others ... to be self-expressive, to be free" (cited in Miller, 1987, p. 238). It was not enough to fight for material gains; social processes had to touch the personal. Breines (1989) summarizes this position as follows:

> The search for and/or struggle to defend community, both the "sense" of community and actual community institutions, becomes political in the context of the changes that capitalism has brought in the everyday life of the individual—changes characterized by lack of control at work school and play; impersonality and competition in all areas of life. (p. 7)

In the creation of new community-based organization in the years that followed, the emphasis on participation and process was the source of democratic innovation that shaped many new practices. A criticism of the concept of prefiguration is that it is utopian and therefore is not something that can be incorporated in the daily struggles for specific gains, which by necessity are shaped by more pragmatic practices. However, in its refinement over the years, the quest for democracy in the everyday helped to shape many new forms of organizing and bequeathed a powerful legacy.

A second challenge for the New Left was that of agency. Here we get into the core of the differences between the old and the New Left. The old left believed that the working class, through its parties in either revolutionary or parliamentary incarnations, was the vehicle for basic change, and that class struggle was the motor that drove social reform. Following the critique of Mills, Marcuse, and others, the New Left saw the working class as integrated into North American materialism and the consumer society (Miller, 1987). The period of affluence had allowed industrial workers to make many gains and created a period of relative stability. It was not uncommon to find unionized workers living in suburbs and enjoying the benefits of consumerism. Unions had become a vehicle for the protection of their members' narrow material interests. The New Left in the United States did not see the trade union movement or the political party it supported—the Democratic Party—as having a commitment to any kind of radical social change. The organizations themselves were hierarchical and did not support the radical democracy that the New Left sought. In Canada, the New Left was divided on this question. As Laxer (1996) points out, many followed the orientation of activists from the USA:

> Youthful activists sought to politicize the poor in community organizing programs that were replicas of programs south of the border—as though Canada had no political traditions or unique social characteristics and values. (pp. 149–50)

However, others challenged the social democrats in the New Democratic Party from within. In 1969, a group of young activists from English Canada, known as the Waffle, prepared a manifesto that promoted Canadian nationalism and challenged American control of Canada. The clash of political cultures and ideas eventually led to the expulsion of the Waffle from the NDP, but their ideas influenced the party and contributed to a rebirth of Canadian nationalism (Laxer, 1996). Thus, both the ideas from the USA, with its anti-party, direct action perspective, and the traditions of a parliamentary left shaped the practices and strategies of the New Left in Canada. The biggest difference between the two countries had to do with the role of the working class as agents of social change.

This was a dilemma that is difficult to resolve in theory and even more complex in practice. The New Left in the USA witnessed and participated in the civil rights movement in the United States in the early 1960s. Black communities in the south challenged segregation and exclusion and won concessions through direct action. At the same time, students in both countries were engaged in a struggle against the "multiversity" that they analyzed as serving corporate interests. They were demanding a voice and control of that institution. The common ground was the concept of participatory democracy. The struggle for social and economic justice, shared with the old left, was not adequate unless the institutions themselves were fundamentally democratized. The majority of people, the New Left believed, had no real voice and lived in the pretense of democracy. The quest for power to shape their own lives and the institutions that touched them was the key element that the New Left believed could bring together many disenfranchised groups (Miller, 1987). The process of democratizing all aspects of society was the means and strategy to challenge the wider society. Even with its attempt to engage in the NDP, the New Left held on to these basic values.

The leading journal of the New Left in Canada was *Our Generation*. It began as a disarmament journal in the early 1960s, and it was a voice of the development of the New Left and subsequently anarchist and libertarian left thought and analysis. An editorial in 1969 articulated the rejection of prevailing political and social institutions as having the potential to change society. Further, agency was understood as a broad-based radical movement. The editors wrote,

> The traditional agencies of political change are failing, and so have the older definitions of politics.... We have no alternative but to withdraw our allegiance from the machines of the electoral process, from the institutions of "representative democracy" like parliaments to forego the magical rite of voting for our freedom, and resume our own initiatives before liberal corporatism asphyxiates us. We are now in a period of transition like the system itself, in which we will seek to unite radicals, in new forms of resistance and counter-institutional building ... we wish to create a political movement of people with the capacity to determine their own lives. (*Our Generation*, 1969, p. 15)

The editorial continues and calls for the building of an "Extra-Parliamentary Opposition" that would bring together people and groups that shared a common critique and minimal program. Although it called for a broad-based movement, the leadership of the more radical wing would come from

> the new left student and youth movement which demands that producers control what they produce using the operational principles of ... "participatory or direct democracy." ... They seek to organise new centers of power among ethnic and racial minorities, urban and rural workers, youth, the poor, and other groups on a neighbourhood and work level. (p. 16)

The New Left understood leadership and agency in different terms than the traditional left. It did not believe in social change through parliamentary channels and it did not confer on one group—the working class—the "leadership" role in social struggles. Building power and gaining a voice was inclusive and needed the participation of many.

Following these beliefs, some activists in the New Left in the USA decided to move off campus and engage in community organizing in low-income communities as a new way to extend their political action. The Students for a Democratic Society (SDS) set up the Economic Research and Action Project (ERAP) in 1963. Its brochure stated,

> We have chosen to work with people who most desperately need alternatives to poverty and economic voicelessness, and to devote ourselves to the development of community organization capable of achieving a better deal for the poor in a democratic fashion. (cited in Breines, 1989, p. 125)

One of the most committed and effective organizers from that time, Susan Jeffery, reflected on her experience:

> I wanted to organize people, I wanted to organize a movement. I mean, on some level it was stupid: we were going to organize the "lumpen," it wasn't Marxist at all, we were going after people who were totally disenfranchised and disempowered and disorganized at a personal level. But we wanted to be independent. We wanted to have a major impact on American society. So we had to carve out an arena in which there wasn't yet an organization. (Miller, 1987, p. 190)

The New Left thus sought new constituencies, particularly those that had not benefited from the post-war boom. In an essay reflecting on the experience of the SDS, Todd Gitlin argued that the poor had many unmet needs and were least tied to the dominant values of the system, and therefore had the potential to work for radical social change (Teodori, 1969). Thus the New Left saw community organizing as having the potential to bring poor people together for a common project—the transformation of society. Teodori (1969) summarizes the position as follows:

the movements suggest a political-organizational praxis which is based on the following criteria: (a) decentralization and multiplicity of structures and actions which serves the movements, and not vice versa; (b) direct method of self-government at all levels, rather than delegated authority and responsibility; (c) abolition of institutionalized political bureaucracies and of the division of political labor between leaders and those who carry out the leadership's policy; (d) nonexclusion. (p. 37)

Each project was to have its autonomy with local leadership. The hope was that, through the building of local power and a longer-term social and political vision, alliances for radical social change could come together.

Fisher (1994) summarizes some of the principles that guided the organizing efforts:

1. Be a catalyst not a leader—the role of the organizer was to facilitate social processes and not lead the community. Local people were to play that role.
2. The key slogan of the period was "let the people decide."
3. Develop loose organizational structures that can maximize participation of the people. Linked to this was an emphasis on consensus decision-making.
4. Establish places in the community free of external restraints. The idea was to create a "community union" that could belong to neighbourhood people.
5. Develop indigenous leaders. This principle is linked to the second, and sees the organizer as a person, who is in the background, so that local people could represent themselves.
6. Create personal relationships. The organizer was to build "Supportive, noncompetitive relations between organizers and community people [that] would prefigure future ways of relating in the new truly democratic society." (pp. 109–10)

New Left organizers carried these principles into the field. In the USA they worked in urban ghettoes attempting to build local organizations. They did not find the reality as easy as the theory. The attempts at internal democratic process were time-consuming and tiring while the issues that they could manage at the local level seemed trivial. The community union approach organized people around specific grievances such as problems of garbage, traffic, or late welfare checks (Breines, 1989). Tom Hayden (1988) describes the work of one project in Newark, New Jersey. Neighbourhood blocks were the units that were organized for this project. They worked on local issues and supported the development of local leaders. He states,

> In a few weeks, we had 250 people meeting in about fifteen block groups. We began knitting them into a neighbor-hood-wide organization so that people from each block could see their problems in larger perspective. We held weekly meetings of block leaders, which led to a neighborhood leadership body. We opened a storefront office on a seven day basis. Soon our mimeos were pouring out leaflets announcing meetings and demonstrations or outlining in simple terms such subjects as tenants' rights and where to get legal aid. (p. 132)

Many of these efforts met with initial success, but they were hard to sustain. Further, with the escalation of the Vietnam War and urban revolt in the US ghettos in the late 1960s, the organizing efforts were derailed. However, their principal ideas and methods influenced many who stayed in the field.

In Canada, the organizing followed similar patterns with young people working among the poor. Poor peoples' organizations were founded in major cities, along with new "counter-institutions" such as community clinics. A government program that was designed to give young people an outlet for their newly acquired social activism supported these projects. The Company of Young Canadians (CYC) was launched in the mid-1960s as a nationwide project to support grassroots community organizing. It had a controversial history, living a tension between promoting social change and falling under the control of the bureaucracy in Ottawa (Brodhead, Goodings, and Brodhead, 1997). The move into community organizing did not go unchallenged from within the New Left. These challenges were at many different levels. One anecdote is particularly illustrative of the division. Two New Left leaders were walking on a street in Montreal when one chastised the other's participation in CYC by reminding him that the state would not finance the revolution (Daly, 1970). This tension between using opportunities that were available even if they presented political dangers versus adopting an uncompromising stance differentiated those who felt that it was possible to make gains by working in and through "the system" and those who wanted to stay the revolutionary course. Once entering into the struggles of a local community, it became much more difficult to ignore the pragmatic tugs of the specific problems that had to be solved. For those who stayed on the radical side of the debate, this was a tension that could not be easily resolved in the daily life of organizing.

Another tension emerged with the practice of participatory democracy. The New Left was anti-leadership and believed that "the people" should decide, but community organizers came from privileged backgrounds, were educated, and had time to reflect on what they were doing. "The people" were brought in afterwards; they were to be organized. There was a real power differential linked to a culture that gave greater credibility to those who were articulate and educated. In practice, power was informal and hidden and there was little formal accountability for the organizers. Richard Rothstein suggested that the way to solve this problem was to put "formal powers in the hands of community people, in other words, reinstituting formal structure" (cited in Breines, 1989, p. 81) This lesson was learned and, as practice developed in the years that followed, structures were put in place that acknowledged the role of organizers and demanded their accountability.

By the late 1960s, women increasingly challenged some of the patriarchal practices in the New Left. Women who participated in community organizing felt this more acutely because while the most effective organizers tended to be women and most local issues sprang from the domestic sphere (Breines, 1989), the most visible organizers tended to be men. The shared oppression of women and the developing feminist consciousness provided a natural bridge between woman organizers and poor women in the community. These themes will be developed later in the chapter.

Another challenge raised the limits of localism. Critics charged that community organizing could not break through its local focus and therefore would not build a radical program that would place the class question at its centre. Further, the central issue of redistribution of wealth could not be challenged from the local level (Breines, 1989). This issue is not unlike the critique of Alinsky organizing, but it takes the question further. A Marxist analysis was beginning to take shape within the New Left. Its focus on class raised difficult questions for those engaged in local work. The longer-term goals of fundamental social change were shared between those working in the community and those advocating workers' revolution, but community organizing was often trapped by the day-to-day demands of working locally. This often clouded the longer-term vision. The counter-argument was that local organizing raised the basic question of democracy, unmasked the realities of how power operated, and provided the opportunity for direct participation and power. These in turn created the conditions which, according to Fruchter and Kramer, "create, then enlarge, a space in which the possible alternatives can be developed, and the possible challenge to the status quo can be kept alive" (cited in Breines, 1989). This debate is the central one, and perhaps is more important in the current context in which opposition forces to a common right-wing and neo-liberal agenda are weak. Local organizing might not win great battles but it can create autonomous democratic places from which mobilization and political organizing are possible.

Many of the projects in that period were innovative and laid foundations for initiatives that followed. However, the actual day-to-day organizing did not depart from the Alinsky approach; both involved building local power by means of a popular organization and gaining concessions through the use of pressure tactics. However, there were also differences. The organizers did not define themselves as professionals but as movement activists. They tried to share, as much as possible, the communities and situations of the people that they were trying to organize. The New Left believed strongly that the organizations put in place were part of a wider social movement working for fundamental social change, and therefore that political education was part of the agenda—exposing basic inequalities and injustices. The movement, as it was called then, had many components; organizing locally was only one part that shared common aims and analysis. The way that loose networks would come together was never clear.

Organizing was directed outward. It was a process of societal change; local gains, although not incidental, were considered a means and were less important than the longer struggle. Thus, the organizers in particular identified with a wider process and were strongly connected to an international movement that was blossoming in the 1960s. The organizational form taken was supposed to be non-hierarchical and participation was to be encouraged in an open process. In contrast, Alinsky-type organizations were highly structured. The New Left raised the organizational question not only in theory but also in practice, with an experimental energy that tried to expand democratic participation into all aspects of daily life.

Two related and underlying concepts shaped the practice, and perhaps these are the most important legacies of the period. Prefiguration and parallel organizations went together in practice. The belief that people had to "live the revolution" shaped the direct democratic participation, not only in community organization but also in struggles on campus. It was not uncommon for students to hold mass decision-making meetings open to all those who wanted to participate. Granted, this was chaotic, but it extended the democratic process and this was the objective. The experimentation with new democratic forms was carried forward into the building of "parallel" organizations that integrated the organizational approach with a service. Examples of these in Quebec and elsewhere were the many services put in place by and with those who used them. In Montreal, in the late 1960s, community clinics—for example, the one in Pointe St. Charles discussed earlier—were established in working-class communities and in areas where the counterculture gathered. The leadership was an alliance of young professionals influenced by the student left and local community activists (Shragge, 1990). Parallel institutions were democratic instances jointly controlled by local citizens and radical professionals contributing to both the provision of a service and the opening of democratic space. At the same time, workers, volunteers, and users of these services continued to participate in a variety of political and social struggles. Service was not divorced from political action.

The organizing efforts initiated by the New Left on both sides of the border represent the beginning of a new type of activism. Struggles have taken new forms, influenced by the underlying beliefs of the 1960s. At the end of the 1960s, many saw the end of a brief period of youth activism. In the USA, the violence and repression polarized the movement, with many advocating armed resistance and others supporting more moderate approaches. In Canada, there was continuity. Government programs tightened the funding available for social experimentation (Keck and

Fulks, 1997), but organizing continued. In both countries, there was a growth of Marxist organizations and many activists entered factories as their place of struggle. Several important tendencies emerged from the New Left, often more quietly and with less drama. I will look at three examples of continuity: new populism and urban activism, women's organizing and services, and social movements.

## CONTINUITIES AND DEVELOPMENTS

Starting in the 1970s, some activists who had worked on projects in the late 1960s turned their energies to more systematic community organizing practice. They brought with them some of the radicalism of the student movement, but they also developed a practice that was more systematic and had an understanding that the revolution was not around the corner and community organizing was a long-term commitment. Throughout the 1970s, many initiatives emerged at the local level. Examples included the organizing of disenfranchised groups such as welfare recipients. In the USA, organizing of welfare recipients created the National Welfare Rights Organization (NWRO). As I described in the first chapter, one of my first grassroots experiences was helping to set up a NWRO chapter. The work was door-to-door and combined education about rights with advocacy and local leadership development. Similar initiatives took place in Canada, such as GMAPCC, but a national organization based on a local chapter structure was never put in place. The continuities with the New Left were the emphasis on supporting local leadership and on creating organizations that allowed direct participation of poor people. The goal was to build a movement of the poor. Although gains were made, the welfare-receiving poor were too small a constituency to build the kind of movement that could go beyond the specific questions that touched that group.

Activists in the 1970s also turned to neighbourhood organizing. The goals of "neo-Alinsky" organizing is described by Fisher (1994) as follows:

> to develop mass political organizations rooted in neighbor-
> hoods, grounded in local concerns, and focused on winning

concrete gains. The goal was to advance social and economic
democracy, empower people, and challenge power relations in
and beyond the neighborhood. (p. 146)

The assumption was this could be accomplished only with a "majoritarian
strategy" that would include those of low and moderate incomes. In the
USA, this strategy was expressed through the founding of many new initiatives. For example, Heather Booth, a former SDS activist, established
the Mid-West Academy to train community organizers. Populist organizations were informed and inspired by long traditions in the USA; those
using these traditions argued for a widening of democracy and power for
people (Evans and Boyte, 1992). ACORN, discussed later in the chapter,
was one of the longest lasting and most significant of these organizations.
The connections between the 1960s and these periods are clear. The
SDS's belief in grassroots democracy and direct action organizing took
root in these populist practices.

In Montreal, the organizing institute with which I was affiliated
during the years 1974 to 1978 organized poor people following a welfare
rights model. Feeling they had reached the limits of this approach, organizers went through a period of reflection about strategy. There were a
number of reasons why they thought that working with the welfare poor
was dead-ended. They thought that those receiving welfare benefits were
too small a group to have a lot of social power. Those who were working
for low wages and those receiving unemployment benefits often shared
many of the same issues as those on welfare and their participation would
broaden the base. In addition, the organizers began to adhere to a traditional class analysis, as did many activists in Quebec at the time. Building
working-class power was the objective. Local organizing was part of
a wider movement for basic social change that included a trade union
movement that had shifted to the left during that period. The organizing
was similar to the Alinsky model, but with attempts to bring organizations
from different neighbourhoods together on common issues. In addition,
there was a concerted effort made to undertake political education, exposing the power relations of the wider society. The context supported
the organizers to move in that direction as a strong left-wing current ran
through community and popular organizations at that time.

Glenn Drover and I (1979) wrote an article reflecting on that practice. We were critical of the process of organization-building and maintenance that required both financial support from outside agencies and a professional cadre of organizers who had indirect control over the organizing processes. We raised the following questions: "Can these struggles lead to alternative visions, and a serious challenge to capitalist hegemony or will they be played out within the dominant framework of reform?" (Drover and Shragge, 1979, p. 69) Perhaps we were asking too much of neighbourhood organizing, but nonetheless we proposed three directions that we thought would contribute to a more radical/socialist alternative. The points included a critique of organization, a need to examine the disruptive power of community organizations, and the building of local alternative organizations. The debate reflects the differences between the populist or neo-Alinsky perspective and a socialist perspective, as well as the tension between those two visions—reformist and Marxist.

The New Left began to fragment by the beginning of the 1970s. Some activists continued to follow the orientations of the earlier periods—namely, an open radical stance with influences from a variety of sources. The organizing work continued with neo-Alinsky populism, but with clear influences of the older left traditions such as anarchism. Others became involved in Marxist groups following Trotskyist traditions or Maoism. The main practice of the latter was to work in factories as a way to politicize and mobilize the working class. However, another shift was to have a longer-term impact and shape the struggles that followed. New social movements, particularly women's and ecology movements, in many ways reshaped social action by taking it out of the community base and finding new expressions for opposition. I will not attempt to cover all aspects of this subject area because it is too vast, but I will examine several dimensions that have contributed in substantial and innovative ways to community organizing practice.

The contributions of feminism to community organizing shared some of the ideas associated with the early New Left, discussed above. The feminist movement was able to both effectively put principles into practice and to build theories from the practice that would reinforce the work of the movement. The ideas that I will present do not necessarily represent the ideas of the whole movement, which is made up of many different groups and tendencies categorized by liberal, radical, and socialist

(Adamson et al., 1988). Liberal feminism focuses on equal opportunities for women through the reform of existing structures. Radical feminism is derived from the biological differences between men and women and argues for a society based on female, life-giving values including cooperation, challenges to hierarchy, and anti-militarism, thus building a women-centred culture and corresponding organizations. Socialist feminism locates women's oppression through the interaction of four elements: gender, class, race, and sexual orientation. It also links these dimensions to the wider structure of the economy and challenges the power based on all of these dimensions, while arguing for fundamental change within them. Adamson, Briskin, and McPhail (1988) go further in differentiating between strategies for change that are institutionalized and those that are grassroots. The former operate and work for change within the institutions of society such as government and political parties, while the latter are community-based, involve collective organizing, reach out to women "on the street," and work at raising consciousness.

It is at the level of the grassroots that women introduced significant innovation to community organizing. One of the departures and important lessons for practice that followed was the understanding that one must look beyond traditional organizations and parliamentary processes as vehicles for social change. Rather, according to Adamson et al. (1988), social change can be promoted through "popular collective movements." They argue that

> Collective action is the extension of the belief in the collective. Collective action as a route to change empowers people in the face of their individual powerlessness. It encourages the active, ongoing participation of large numbers and the pooling of resources by marginalized groups usually excluded from formal political power, and validates both our right and our power to change not only ourselves, but the world around us.... participation on collective action is often the route to individual change. (p. 155)

A central principle that crystallized in feminism is that the personal cannot be separated from the political. Social struggle implies personal change and personal change encourages social engagement. The joining of the public and private spheres was a big step forward. For example, the struggles around reproductive rights and domestic violence followed and contributed to the strengthening of this practice. In terms of the organizing process, Adamson et al. (1988) argue that

> the connection between personal problems and public solutions did more than direct women's attention towards the overall social change: it also helped to break down the numbing isolation of personal experience and to activate women politically. (p. 201)

These lessons were central for other identity-based movements such as ones based on disability or sexual orientation. These movements grew in size as individuals redefined personal oppression in political terms that encouraged others to feel safe doing the same. The organizing discussed earlier concerns a process in which one group—the organizers, the politicos—organizes others—usually the poor, the working class, and so on. The women's movement and those that followed began with organizing on a personal level, seeing how their own issues are shared by others in similar circumstances, and then trying to do something about it. The form of organizing also changed; organizers were now part of the process. They were not outsiders who did not necessarily live the issues. Because it was a social movement, practice went beyond single organizations, linkages were established between diverse types of organizations and practice, and struggling for common objectives was forged. The capacity to mobilize and to educate people beyond the membership of a particular group created strength. Participation was inclusive of many perspectives and practices. New organizations were put in place that carried forward the values and practices of the movement—the creation of a democratic space and the support of solidarity between women.

However, like other social movements and groups, there were debates about strategy. Briskin (1991) summarizes two positions that emerge from within the women's movement: disengagement and mainstreaming. The former, she argues, "operates from a critique of the system and a standpoint outside of it, and a desire, therefore, to create alternative structures and ideologies" (p. 30). By contrast, the latter "operates from a desire to reach out to the majority of the population with popular and practical

feminist solutions to particular issues" (p. 30). She argues that the movement requires both and that each has its risks. "Disengagement can lead
to marginalization and invisibility; mainstreaming to co-optation and
institutionalization" (Briskin, 1991, p. 31). The creation of alternatives
was a strong feature of the feminist movement. These included shelters
for women subjected to violence, rape crisis centres, and a variety of community and collective projects that brought women together. At the same
time, campaigns for improvements to their situations, such as access to
abortion, led to important victories. The tension discussed by Briskin is
present in a variety of other places in the community movement. Groups
try to create their own services and projects that build a place in which
they have control and a defining voice. But at the same time, will the
energy spent on these activities isolate groups—and, perhaps more importantly, will it mitigate against their participation in wider mobilization
and political engagement?

The women's movement took the organization question further than
the New Left and put into practice new forms of service provision. These
challenged the dominant division between professional and client, and
they were managed through collective processes. Ristock (1991) describes
the organizations as follows:

> Collective practices for the delivery of services, internal
> processes, and perceptions of work reflect a consistency
> between their organizational structure and feminist princi-
> ples. Identifying hierarchical, bureaucratic organizations as
> perpetuating a power imbalance in our society, they remain
> committed to consensus decision-making practices. They have
> adopted the egalitarian principle that each worker is used ac-
> cording to her own strengths, and not according to educational
> background. (p. 43)

She discusses some of the difficulties and contradictions that have been
faced by feminist collectives. Despite these complexities, these types of
organizations create the possibility of democracy as part of everyday life
and give people the opportunity to exercise some control over their work
lives. In addition, the practice took the initial impulse of the New Left
into a realm where the conflicts between ideals and realities had to be

confronted. In many instances it succeeded in successfully building a tradition that combined a democratic form of organization with service provision and involvement with social struggles. I will examine some of the contradictions of these forms later in this book, but here, I want to acknowledge the positive and innovative contributions of the women's movement, and the links that it has with some of the ideas of the early New Left.

Finally, I want to discuss some of the characteristics of social movements as they evolved in the 1970s and 1980s as having continuity with the New Left. There is a vast literature that analyzes these movements, but I will not explore that here. Rather, I want to describe some of the forms of action that have been developed. A tradition of direct action continues, influenced less by community organizing than by the peace and other social movements. Noël Sturgeon (1995) describes these as "nonviolent direct action movements" that are "extra-institutional." Their identifying characteristics include the use of affinity groups, consensus forms of decision-making, and tactics that include direct confrontation and civil disobedience. Campaigns such as those against nuclear weapons and nuclear power, those against forms of discrimination, and those supporting resistance to the institutions of trade liberalization have been conducted through these forms of direct action. The affinity groups are a central aspect and remind me of the attempt of the community organizers from ERAP to build community for themselves while engaging in struggles for wider social change. Affinity groups, according to Sturgeon (1995),

> form a decentralized organizational structure that minimizes bureaucracy and formal leadership, consistent with the antihierarchical proclivities of the movement.... the members of the affinity group construct an obligation to each other that is based only on their participation in consensus process and their mutual political action.... [It] serves as a symbol of an alternative political order intended to be placed against the straight lines and hierarchical structures of police barricades and military facilities. (p. 39)

These social movements do not take the form of traditional organizations but they might receive support from existing organizations as allies. They are based on the assumption that mass mobilization is the best expression of opposition and that this is best expressed through direct confrontation. The relationship between social movements and community organizing is symbiotic. Each contributes to the health of the other, but they are different. Social movements tend to have a period of growth and decline and then a rebirth. Community organizing tends to be encapsulated in an organizational form with specific mandates and staff. The principle of an organization is that it can overcome the unstable nature of social movements. But, as we discussed earlier, it is difficult to sustain the momentum of the more radical aspects of these organizations over time.

## COMMUNITY ACTION: CONCLUDING COMMENTS

I will return to the questions that I raised earlier in the chapter. The first question examined the relationship of context to practice—the opportunities and the constraints. There are several important factors that contributed to community action organizing's ability to develop in the late 1960s and 1970s. The combination of a growing economy, an active interventionist government, and the presence of social movements including the student/youth left interacted in tension. The governments in both the USA and Canada were in the midst of a period of social reform. In the USA it was in response to the civil rights movement and urban unrest, while in Canada there was a strong trade union movement, a nationalist movement in Quebec with a left-wing orientation, and a strong, radical youth movement. Part of both governments' response was to "cool out" the more radical edge by drawing participation into their sanctioned programs and directing dissent towards established channels. In order to do this, at least at its initial stages, there was flexible and decentralized funding for different types of activities. The double conditions that supported organizing were the social movements that provided the base, which contested aspects of the wider society; and the money that was trying to direct these actions into "safer" directions. The results were opportunities to expand an action strategy. At the same time, this was a constraint. A reliance on state programs and money and the normal rise and fall of social movements were weaknesses that resulted in the demise of some of the action organizing. However, as I tried to demonstrate, there was continuity in the ideas and practices of the earlier period through to the social movements of today. Thus, even though the earlier period did not make the dramatic gains that had been envisioned, the legacy and contribution was passed down the line to other activists and movements.

Two interrelated issues are the social vision of this period as well as its contribution to practice and the processes of practice. I will discuss these together. There are different visions and these did not always enter into day-to-day organizing activities with any coherence. The organizing influenced by Alinsky and his followers believed that it was possible, within the political system, for citizens to represent their interests through organization-building coupled with pressure tactics. There was an inherent belief in the openness of the state to accommodate, albeit reluctantly, the demands of these groups. In contrast, the New Left and the social movements that followed had an explicit critique of the system and sought fundamental change, at least in theory. The problem was that effective practice was also defined by the winning of concessions. The tensions, then, are between the vision and the practice, and in the problem of connecting the two. There were a couple of ways that this was done. First, the question of the form of organization was accorded central importance both in the organizing attempts of the New Left and in the social movements that followed. Organizing was about building a democratic community in which all members could have a voice. It was to be a democratic space based on direct participation. Through the challenging of traditional notions of democracy—representation—and by substituting more direct forms, organizers believed that this would contribute to a process of social and political empowerment and spill over into other aspects of peoples' lives. This would in turn lead to other changes and processes in both public institutions and private lives. In the course of organizing, what messages are conveyed to participants? The New Left and other social movements contributed to a critical social analysis while working for specific changes. Consciousness-raising, introduced by the women's movement, was designed to link personal experiences of oppression with a political understanding of the wider relations of power and domination. This is diffuse, but it is central, and it contributes to the creation of a culture of opposition. Community organizing can contribute to it through supporting and encouraging a critical analysis that links the specific issues to political and social processes as well as the relations of power. Further, another important condition is forging connections to other similar organizations, campaigns, and social movements. In other words, community organizations cannot remain isolated but need to build solidarity with others. Without these links, community organizations can end up retreating into their own "backyards" and remaining isolated. If there is any conclusion that can be drawn, it is that there is no conclusion. Community action organizing from Alinsky to contemporary social movements shares similarities and differences. Organizing can work for all of the ideologies Fisher discussed above, from reactionary through to radical. The challenge for those struggling for progressive change is to understand how to use the tools and traditions that can contribute to the end goals of progressive social change. The next chapter will examine how the community movement lost sight of its critical edge and, through its expertise and professionalism, successfully became an extension of state-defined services and development.

# CHAPTER FOUR

# SOCIAL ACTION CONTINUES:
# FIGHTING BACK IN A NEO-LIBERAL AGE

In the previous edition of the book, I ended the discussion of social action at the end of the previous chapter. I presented the action model as dominant in the 1960s and 1970s but declining as other approaches (which will be discussed in the next chapter) superseded the politicized direction of community action. In order to discuss the continuity of community action, I will describe several different organizations and present some of their similarities and some of their differences. The organizations all have had a long history, often going back at least twenty years. These include ACORN, Front d'action populaire en réaménagement urbain (FRAPRU), and Industrial Areas Foundation (IAF). The organization called the Right to the City Alliance is more recent but many of its member organizations have been around for twenty years or more. Returning to the chapter on models, all of these examples fit into the action model. The differences are in whether these organizations lean towards the integration or the oppositional side of the models. In practice, as we will see, it is more complicated. All of them adhere to the underlying principle that people acting collectively can gain power and win victories that improves their lives. However, three of them—ACORN, the Right to the City Alliance, and FRAPRU—all act to build opposition to the neo-liberal foundations of contemporary capitalism.

# INDUSTRIAL AREAS FOUNDATION (IAF)

The IAF was founded by Alinsky in 1940 to support and extend his organizing to other communities, and today it continues his legacy and his approach. In the current period, the IAF has grown to include over fifty affiliated organizations (Lynch, 2005–2006), mainly in the USA but with others in Canada and the UK. Alinsky's approach was to build organizations of organizations as a means to increase local power. Many of these were churches. The Catholic Church supported Back of the Yards, his first organization founded in Chicago in 1939, but at the same time the organization had a strong affiliation with trade unions and other local recreational and ethnic associations. Because of the central role played by these organizations in the daily lives of people and because of the legitimacy of their leaders, a council of organizations was the first step in building power at the local level. In the current period, congregational or faith-based organizing has become the "religion" of the IAF. One IAF organizer stated that IAF organizers "begin by establishing relations with the enduring community institutions … churches and synagogues and civic associations" (cited in Lynch, 2005–2006, p. 573). The IAF organizations have made gains at the local level—for example, a living wage victory in Baltimore, subsidized housing in Brooklyn, and school improvements in Texas (Warren, 2001). One of the central remaining precepts of Alinsky organizing is that it is "non-ideological." Pragmatic approaches and working to make concrete gains though organizations pressuring authorities are at its core. Perhaps this is the reason that the IAF succeeded in reaching people through faith-based organizing.

However, there is an underlying ideology, and that is a belief that democracy in the USA can be repaired to work for the majority. Mark Warren (2001) provides an articulate overview of how IAF works in its organizing process along with its underlying beliefs. IAF prioritizes the rebuilding of the democratic process in the USA and remedying the way that it has become disconnected from citizens. "Stable institutions of community life" (Warren, 2001, p. 15) are the basis for connecting people to the political process. The strategy is to target faith-based organizations, not individuals. Individuals become active and take on leadership roles through these organizations. The beginning step is described as "relational organizing" through meetings that discuss the needs of the

community and build leadership through issues that arise from these discussions. The goal is to "generate power to back up community demands
through the support of member institutions and the relational organizing in community networks" (Warren, 2001, p. 33). The approach is a
mixture of building power to counter the lack of accountability of the
political system and a mainstreaming of organizing within the political
system as it is. In some ways the approach is a continuity of what Alinsky
did in Back of the Yards in Chicago in 1939, but the rhetoric is more
moderate and the agenda less challenging. In 2001, Warren was writing
at a moment in which there was a critique of the globalized economic
structure, international financial institutions playing a more active role,
and a movement that was in the streets challenging this new phase of
capitalist economic development. To analyze the problem as the lack of a
functioning democracy, and to see the role of community organizations
as mediating bodies while decisions were increasingly removed from local
politics, demonstrates the limited analysis and vision. Certainly, in that
period, alliances with wider movements (see Fisher and Shragge, 2000)
and a deeper analysis would have helped move the politics beyond the
local while understanding the forces—like the global economy—that
shape the local. As important as it is to enter into alliances and contribute
to a wider movement, building a local base and leadership is essential—
but limited. Both the success and limits of IAF's organizing rest on its
localism. Despite having many affiliates, they have not built strategies
and practices that go beyond their local work. Towards the end of his
life in the early 1970s, Alinsky argued, prophetically, that a broad-based
movement that aligned the poor and the middle class was necessary to
counter the movement to the right in the USA. IAF has not taken up this
challenge and local organizations remain local. Further, their "non-ideological" stance is in practice an ideology. Essentially, it is a belief in political pluralism, in the sense that pressure groups can work themselves
into the system and that community organizations are the means to do so.
There is no analysis of what limits exist, nor of how changing organizing
strategies and perspectives can help in challenging these limits. Going
back to the first chapter and the table, IAF represents an approach that
combines social action and social integration.

## ACORN

ACORN comes out of the tradition of Alinsky organizing and elements of the New Left described earlier in this chapter.[1] It began in 1970 in Little Rock as a single community-based effort and has expanded over thirty-five years in the USA into a federated organization, the Association of Community Organizations for Reform Now (ACORN), which at its peak had 100 affiliated community locals with more than 175,000 members. It closed as an organization in 2010, partly due to internal conflicts and as result of concerted attacks from the right-wing media and politicians, and manipulated scandals (Atlas, 2010). Many of member organizations of ACORN have reconstituted and continue to work under other names and without a USA-wide organization. In addition, ACORN International has exported the model to Canada and countries in Asia and Latin America. In contrast to IAF, ACORN's strategy is direct grassroots organizing, building chapters by going door to door, recruiting membership, and building leadership.

ACORN developed a "majoritarian strategy" to target low- and moderate-income Americans in order to build a broader based organization and a more effective mass movement. With its roots in Alinsky-style organizing, it pursued this with a combination of pragmatism and New Left populism. The goal was to force targets—increasingly in the private sector, but also public bodies—to address issues concerning their membership and win victories that build the organization and further broader movement objectives of social, economic, and political justice. There was an activist character to the organization that connected to the legacy of prior social movements and an implicit and explicit critique of mainstream dominant institutions, structures, and power arrangements; and there was an effort to offer an oppositional alternative to ruling groups and the status quo. ACORN also engaged in electoral politics by supporting candidates, organizing the Working Families Party, and participating in voter registration derives. While many social action organizations were turning exclusively to service and development after 2000, ACORN caught a "second wind" at that point and continued to expand, both in its membership and its local chapters.

---

1 The material on ACORN, in addition to that cited, is derived from collaboration with Bob Fisher.

ACORN's model required that individuals pay dues and be part of a national network of federated local chapters with national leadership and professional staff. The local-national relationship led to ACORN's ability to run campaigns across the USA, mobilizing its chapters and membership to target large corporations. One example was ACORN's taking on the tax preparation company H&R Block (Fisher, Brooks, and Russell, 2009). Their primary tactic was to hold highly visible protests at H&R Block offices located in the same poor communities of people of colour in which ACORN organized. They mobilized members to protest in front of these local offices on specific days, which pressured the company. The protesters denounced predatory practices. They were successful and won not only changes in corporate policies but an agreement to allow ACORN to provide tax services for its members. This leads to the second point—services. As discussed previously, many organizations after 1980 went the route of becoming professional service providers, consequently losing their political and social engagement. ACORN had the vision and ability to use services to increase membership and funding, and to link service to campaigns. For example, along with their campaign demanding that banks invest in local housing (Community Reinvestment), ACORN successfully pressured some of the major banks to pay for its homeownership and home-building programs, and to work with the organization to provide mortgages. In this way, ACORN was able to use these services to connect with their political campaigns, help their membership to receive mortgages, and increase organizational funding at the same time (Drier, 2009). Similar approaches were used in providing tax services. The lesson here is that services do not necessarily lead to less organizing, but can reinforce it and contribute to both organization-building and financial resources.

Even with the events in the USA and ACORN closing its doors, the model continues through ACORN International. Since 2004, ACORN has built chapters in several Canadian cities—Toronto, Ottawa, New Westminster, and Cape Breton. According to its website it has 40,000 members in twenty neighbourhoods across seven cities. Its local organizations build leadership and recruit members on local issues such as housing in Cape Breton, on living wage campaigns in Ottawa and New Westminster, or on campaigns for improved and cheaper public transit and tenant organizing in Toronto. Campaigns have also been launched at the provincial level, including support for a private member's bill in Ontario demanding limits on the fees charged for remittance payments sent to the families of immigrants (see www.acorncanada.org). The local provincial/national framework used in the USA thus continues to be part of activism practice as well as direct recruitment using door-to-door canvassing, leadership-building, and the training and support of emerging leaders. Funding is a balance of membership fees and outside sources such as support from foundations and trade unions. The positive lessons of ACORN's long history in the USA have been exported to Canada and to other countries around the world. The core lesson is that organizing people at the grassroots level can build power, and that local leadership can be the voice of ACORN both locally and nationally.

To conclude, ACORN, despite the internal problems at the end of its existence in the USA, was at the forefront of grassroots organizing. Its contribution is impressive from many vantage points. The number of people touched by the organization, and the large group of leaders and organizers who they trained, have gone on to be at the forefront of many social and political struggles, and they have gained the ability to win substantial victories. Delgado (2009) added up the monetary benefits that ACORN realized between 1995 and 2005, including those won through its living wage campaigns and the victories in its fight against predatory lending, and concluded that members and the wider community gained over $15 billion through their campaigns. This is more impressive when it is viewed in the context of the neo-liberal changes and the general movement of community organizations away from organizing. Ideologically, ACORN would not describe itself as "transformative" or "anti-capitalist," but at the same time their campaigns and struggles are about building power for the working class and the poor, and demanding economic redistribution from the wealthy and powerful. There have been many critiques and criticisms of ACORN, including at times top-down leadership, a lack of clear left-wing ideology, and a tendency to go it alone rather than build coalitions with either social movements or other organizations. However, ACORN has left an important legacy and continues to organize across Canada and across the globe, and many of its organizations in the USA have reappeared under different names.

## RIGHT TO THE CITY ALLIANCE (RTTCA)

The Right to the City Alliance is an impressive grouping of some of the radical community organizations in the USA. It was founded in June of 2007 at a meeting at the United States Social Forum in Atlanta, Georgia. The Alliance sought to build a vision of a radical transformation of city power relations and real democratic practices.

> At the founding conference, The Right to the City Alliance built on this framework and developed principles of unity ... that challenged market-based approaches to urban develop- ment and support for economic justice, environmental justice, immigrant justice, racial justice, and democracy (Goldberg, 2008).

Ideologically and politically the Right to the City developed its basis of unity around broad left politics: land for people (not land for specula- tion); public land ownership; economic justice; Indigenous justice; envi- ronmental justice; freedom from police and state harassment; immigrant justice; services and community institutions; democracy and participa- tion; reparations; internationalism; and rural justice (Perera, 2008). The Right to the City concept is a radical and flexible credo to unite exist- ing, like-minded organizations in a common political cause and vision. Groups invited to join the Alliance shared a left-wing radicalism in their politics, visions, strategies, and tactics. They also shared a focus on build- ing power not simply *with* inner-city people of colour but *by* their non- White base. This included a heavy emphasis on developing leadership among people of colour and mobilizing members as well as delivering outcomes in inner-city communities. Significantly, the founding confer- ence emphasized a theory of change with a broad global perspective.

> They do not believe that the fight for the city can be isolated from broader social dynamics. They connect the fight for the city to the struggles of rural people and indigenous people against environmental degradation and economic pressures, and they believe that the struggle for cities in the United States is connected to international struggles (Goldberg, 2008).

As Marcuse (2009) states, the underlying ideologies are a convergence between necessity and the demand for something better—a connection between the deprived and the discontented. He describes this as "a battle of ideology ... grounded in material oppression but not limited to it, combining the demands of the oppressed with the aspirations of the alienated" (p. 192). Member organizations bridge old and new social movement divides, another element that is all too rare in contemporary organizing.

Hilary Goldberg (2010, pp. 102–4) summarizes below the underlying beliefs of the Alliance and the compatibility among the local groups invited to create the Alliance. The starting point is the fight against neoliberal globalization. This analysis of the context is linked to contemporary consequences of this historical period of capitalism for cities and working-class communities. However, the struggle cannot be confined to one system of oppression; it has to connect the different struggles and to be inclusive of all people who face oppression. The city is a key site for the struggle. This belief recognizes the important role of cities in global capitalism. It draws a parallel between the factory as the site of struggle in early forms of capitalism and the city being that site in the contemporary period. Finally, organizing oppressed people is the heart and soul of the movement. The goal is to build the collective power and leadership of working-class people and people of colour "who are on the frontlines of neoliberalism" (Goldberg, 2010, p. 103). And finally, grass-roots organizing must be combined with deep political analysis.

Currently there are thirty-four registered core member groups in the Alliance. They are concentrated in eight regions, with ten organizations in New York City, five in San Francisco, four in both Boston and Los Angeles, three in both Miami and New Orleans, and two each in DC and Providence. The Alliance organizations are concentrated on the east and west coasts with the exception of New Orleans. Their placement in large, multi-ethnic cities with a history of progressive struggle contributes to a common agenda and framework. The concentration of organizations in particular cities enables citywide campaigns and coalitions in these major centres. This represents an impressive step forward in building beyond the grassroots. Though the restriction of these organizations to a handful of cities limits the Alliance's potential as a national organization, it still challenges the Alliance to coordinate member organizations in different cities, primarily those on the east and west coasts. From the outset a conscious effort was made in the Alliance to invite groups that differed in their origins and history, but which shared and could be united around an oppositional theory and practice. Member organizations brought together traditions from different periods of urban movements.

The oldest organizations in the Alliance—Chinese Progressive Association, San Francisco (1972); City Life/Vida Urbana, Boston (1973); and Chinese Progressive Association, also in Boston (1977)—all grew out of left-wing movements and traditions. However, consistent with new social movement forms, their organizing of working-class people was through neighbourhoods and ethnicity rather than directly in factories, which were the primary sites of old social movement organizing. Both Chinese organizations have a commitment to labour organizing and rights but from a community perspective. City Life/Vida Urbana has strong old and new left dimensions. Four of the Alliance's organizations were founded in the 1980s, including Centro Presente in Somerville, Massachusetts (1981), and the Committee Against Anti-Asian Violence (1986) in New York. Like many of the other members of the Alliance, these groups have integrated a service component into their organizing. The majority of organizations in the Alliance were formed after 1990. They organize in new immigrant communities and are concerned with core issues of housing, urban displacement/gentrification and labour, and a corresponding polarization of wealth and income with an enlarged urban poor working in low-paying jobs. Urban redevelopment plans and mega-projects often result in displacement and contestation about the use of urban space.

The "anti-globalization movement" has influenced both the ways that groups in this period organize themselves and their theories of change. At the level of organization, a new form of organizing beyond the local emerged, influenced by the movement and the United States Social Forum. The anti-globalization mobilization of large demonstrations—for example, Seattle in 1999—is based on autonomous organizations and movements working together with decentralized and horizontal structures and processes. The various forums, which are associated with the World Social Forum, have similar decentralized structures and processes. They bring actors from movements and organizations together; however, the goal is not to build a unified strategy or organization but to share experiences, deepen analysis, and network between groups interested in the same issues. As Goldberg (2008) points out, the United States Social Forum provided the Alliance with a comparable space to reflect on organizing practices and the conditions of cities, and it served as a site where groups developed and shared analysis. The members of the Alliance tend to have either an anti-capitalist, anti-corporate, or at least an anti-neo-liberal analysis, which has been encouraged and supported by the wider social movements that emerged in the period after 1990. Despite the diverse historical roots of Alliance member organizations, both a radical theory of change and openness to new organizational forms have linked local efforts and remain essential building blocks of the Alliance structure. The challenges of migration and related low-wage work, and the dominance of finance capital and the impact it has had on urban development are two of the key challenges that shaped the context of the Alliance members. The post-2000 anti-globalization movement and related social forums have influenced their structure with bottom-up processes in contrast with older traditions of the left based on party leadership and cadres.

The member organizations of the Alliance prioritize a wide range of issues ranging from environment to youth engagement to small-scale business development. The local work demonstrates the orientation to practice that influences the general politics of the wider Alliance organization. Further, the Alliance's structure emphasizes that the autonomy of the member organizations and the wider orientation is thus a bottom-up process of a shared political culture and orientation. Many of the Alliance member organizations bring an explicitly left-wing analysis into their organizational life. They identify the system as neo-liberal capitalism and understand how the nature of the system itself is the source of the issues that they face. Nik Theodore, in an interview with Hugill and Brogan (2011), argues that organizations within the Alliance "have a strong current of popular education that runs through their very core.... they view education as a process of social transformation. It is part of consciousness-raising and leadership development" (p. 4). For example, one of the organizations, POWER, which has been based in San Francisco since 1996 and is involved in organizing many issues, developed a text to explain to members and leaders the role of United States imperialism in creating the social and economic problems linked to migration and poverty (Browne et al., 2005). To build an opposition movement for the long run requires an analysis that situates specific issues in a wider context.

According to their "21st Century Cities—A Strategy to Win," a document that as of this writing is still under consideration by the whole organization,

> To take Right to the City to the next level, the leadership is putting forward a strategy for municipal power to intentionally unite core constituencies with other sectors of the progressive community, progressive labor, and urban environmentalists, toward a program of both defense and pro-actively fighting for the type of cities that will not only benefit our people but provide a way to address the root causes of what is happening. We believe that one of the challenges to our historic work is that we build at neighborhood levels and have rarely been able to be in strategic alliances with partners who brought significant numbers, resources, and political power to the table. (Right to the City Alliance—National Organization, 2011, p. 1)

The Right to the City Alliance was created out of already existing organizations, some with more than twenty years of history. Further, these organizations all came out of different traditions, priorities, and local structures. The basis of their unity is their shared radical practice of community organizing and their analysis of the contemporary context of neo-liberal capitalism and related urban processes and issues. These organizations and the Alliance have been able to combine a critique of contemporary capitalism and political education, and at the same time build a base with local leaders and fight for specific issues. This commitment is a break from the traditions of IAF and ACORN. It is too early to tell what wider impact this relatively new organization will have, but it is clearly building both local power and a wider voice for opposition to the system. It still faces some difficult questions: how to build beyond the local? How can the Alliance unite local efforts into a greater force that can contend for power on a national scale? How does the form of organization chosen by the Alliance affect the possibility of building a national movement and power that contends beyond the local?

# FRAPRU

I will now present an organization from Quebec that has been able to maintain a militant action approach and a strong base in their local communities and beyond. In addition, it has developed a high profile as the leading grassroots organization on issues related to poverty, housing, and urban development. Front d'action populaire en réaménagement urbain (FRAPRU) was founded in 1978, and continues in the tradition of organizing and building power for working-class and poor people in order to challenge government policies that keep many in poverty and badly housed.

FRAPRU is a Quebec-wide "regroupement" or coalition of organizations. It has two types of members: participating groups and associate members. The participating groups have contributed to FRAPRU's strong base. These organizations, twenty-nine in total, are located across Quebec. They are all active in their local communities on the range of housing issues, and they all have a local membership base of tenants, public housing residents, or local residents involved on issues of urban development. This has been one of the aspects of FRAPRU's success— the structure brings together local organizations that have active bases in their local communities and staff to support them. The associate members are community organizations, some unions, and movement organizations such as women's groups from across the province. There are approximately 120 of these members, and this gives FRAPRU very broad-based support and connects the associate members to the issues of housing and urban development.

Over the years, FRAPRU has maintained a clear political and ideological position. Its position challenges neo-liberal beliefs and the growing commodification of housing. The organization believes that housing is a fundamental right, an essential good, and that all people regardless of income and other personal characteristics have a right to it. Housing is a collective right, so it transcends individuals and markets. In addition, the state has a key role to play in guaranteeing this provision. The private market, they argue, cannot meet the housing needs of low-income people. State intervention is necessary to provide and to support social housing cooperatives, non-profit housing, and public housing, and to regulate the private rental market to protect the interests of tenants, particularly those who are low-income. Finally, the organization supports people building collective control of their housing and neighbourhood conditions. Thus, local collective action is at the core of their orientation. The bottom-up approach is reflected in FRAPRU's decision-making process—a federated structure with local member organizations sending delegates to regular assemblies (four times a year) and participating in the annual congress that decides priorities and direction. The combination of local autonomy and a democratically determined organizational direction builds the strength from the bottom but allows a coherent vision and leadership. An elected board of directors serves to coordinate the internal functioning of the organization and is elected from participating members.

FRAPRU comes out of a tradition of tenant organizing and resistance to urban development that displaces working-class neighbourhoods for "progress." In the 1960s and 1970s, leading up the EXPO 67 and the 1976 Olympics in Montreal, the city intensified its "progress," plowing highways through old districts with devastating consequences for working-class and poor neighbourhoods. New social housing was built at the expense of older low-income communities. There was resistance to these projects and in many districts tenants began organizing to challenge the power of private landlords. Thus, when FRAPRU was founded there was already a base for their work and a tradition in working-class neighbourhoods across Quebec. In 1974, the Quebec government adopted a program to accelerate demolition of older working-class districts in the name of revitalization. The program permitted intervention in fifty-seven cities and districts. In 1977 a conference to evaluate this program brought together housing activists and citizens in one Montreal district and it became clear to them that broader action was required. A subsequent meeting in 1978, with 200 people representing twenty-one associations from across the province, adopted a manifesto and created a permanent coalition on the issues of urban development and housing. The founding of this kind of coalition structure with a manifesto for action was not at all unique in that period. The continuity is what is exceptional. It is one of the few coalitions of relatively small grassroots organizations that has not only survived but has continued to play a dynamic leadership role on issues—primarily housing, but also urban development. It continues to mobilize and fight for decent housing for working-class and low-income people. Over the many years of its existence it has led many campaigns and been consistently visible in the streets. I will provide a couple of examples and conclude with some lessons.

As happened to many organizations born in the late 1970s, FRAPRU had to confront ongoing attacks on social gains, whether in the name of a balanced state budget or a wholesale transformation to market-led neo-liberal strategies. In addition, initially there were major cuts in federal spending on housing and finally a complete withdrawal from spending in that area. From the beginning FRAPRU faced huge challenges but, despite the deterioration of public programs, it kept pressuring the federal, provincial, and municipal governments and managed many victories. The following examples illustrate some of its directions. Soon after its founding, FRAPRU and its member groups were engaged in local campaigns for different forms of social housing. In the 1980s, some of their victories included the following: Comité Logement Rosemont and FRAPRU were part of a large coalition to demand and win 2,000 housing units in the redeveloped Angus Rail Yards, and a housing group in Pointe St. Charles gained 500 new housing units. By the 1990s, federal funding was disappearing and finally the federal government under Mulroney withdrew from housing entirely. FRAPRU resisted and protested by organizing occupations, setting up outdoor camps, and educating the general public as well as pressuring the Liberal opposition for policies that would re-engage the federal government in spending on social housing programs. Once that venture ended in failure, FRAPRU targeted the provincial government. Here they met with more success. Local campaigns had been going on during this period, with new social housing projects put in place before the federal cuts set in. In 1994 FRAPRU pressured the opposition, the Parti Québécois (PQ), to make commitments to housing if elected. A variety of tactics were used and the PQ announced a program to buy and renovate buildings for social housing. When elected they brought in this program but delivered less than promised. Even with this disappointment, Quebec remained one of two provinces that had a program of investment in social housing. Even after the referendum defeat, and in the context of austerity, the PQ brought in a program that invested $215 million in social housing over five years. These gains were in many ways a result of the consistent organizing of FRAPRU, which combined lobbying with direct action and continued to enlarge and maintain an active base in local communities.

Over the years, FRAPRU and their member organizations have campaigned, protested, occupied offices, and lobbied for improved housing conditions. They have won victories at all levels. In addition, FRAPRU has been a member of broader coalitions in the fight for justice for low-income people. There are far too many examples to list and discuss here, but they include challenging the city of Montreal on housing shortages for low-income people, continuous pressuring of the provincial and federal governments, and contributing to victories with increased funding for social housing. FRAPRU has been one of the most successful organizations in Quebec over many years. It has learned how to sustain a base through member organizations. At times, some organizations have disbanded or left and others have been recruited. The dynamism of seeking new member groups and allies has paid off over time. Its strength is also derived from acting at different levels without sacrificing one for the other. Local groups have fought battles with landlords on development projects and campaigned for social housing. FRAPRU itself has led or participated in campaigns at all levels. With this local-central dynamic, FRAPRU has become powerful enough to be the primary force in contesting government housing policy and promoting alternatives. Its research and policy analysis play key roles in this process. It has also been tactically creative, drawing on the arts, visual images in public spaces, and theatre to promote its message. At the same time, these tactics are fun for members of the organizations. FRAPRU has been one of the key community-based organizations to contribute ongoing opposition to the direction of government policy and the neo-liberal turn in general. They are on the ground, visible, and they have an active base through member organizations as well as a strong leadership, all of which contributes to their role as an organization that builds opposition and mobilizes for justice.

## CONCLUDING COMMENTS

All four of these organizations share roots with the community action traditions going back to Alinsky, and later with the New Left. Despite changes in the general orientation of community organizations—and with moderate, professional service or development organizations emerging as the dominant approaches—there has been a continuity of this tradition. The organizations discussed all have a conflict perspective, with an analysis of power and a goal of shifting power through collective action by people—be they low-income, working-class, or poor. They all have succeeded in being able to organize and mobilize a membership by maintaining an active local community and supporting leaders. Through this organizing, they have won impressive victories in a difficult socio-economic context. With the exception of IAF, all have developed a structure that has created a base through local work, whether it is an autonomous organization such as FRAPRU and Right to the City Alliance, or ACORN with its more centralized model. These structures have contributed to long-term work. This contrasts many social movements that have appeared and disappeared in the same period, making contributions and mobilizing but not being able to keep going over the longer term. This is one of the advantages of building an organization. The organizations discussed are all based on direct active participation of members—either those formally defined by dues and so on, or informal memberships made up of people affected by the issues coming together to find strategies to change the wider situation. The key is this active participation but there is variation. ACORN and IAF tend towards a formal membership, while organizations with a federated structure like RTTCA and FRAPRU allow more variation in how local groups structure their membership and forms of participation.

One issue that emerges is the leadership within the group of organizers. IAF, ACORN, and FRAPRU have at least one or more organizers who act in a leading role and have been with the organization for most of its history. The lead organizer of IAF, Ed Chambers, was trained by Alinsky and has been there for more than thirty years. The founder and lead organizer of ACORN, Wade Rathke, was with ACORN almost until it closed and he is the lead organizer and founder of ACORN International. The coordinator of FRAPRU, François Saillant, was a founder and coordinator for most of its existence. It is too early to see this pattern with RTTCA but some of the member organizations that have been around for a long time have had stable leadership and organizers as well. The obvious issues are gender and succession. However, there is another dimension: stable leadership and the drive and energy of these lead organizers. In addition, in many of the organizations the daily work brings leadership from many different individuals. The long-term leadership certainly has limits and problems, such as those in ACORN, but at the same time it contributes to the longevity and continuity of these organizations.

Another important aspect is the ideology and understanding of how these organizations contribute to social change. The IAF has chosen to be "non-ideological" and supports local organizing based on needs that are usually defined by lower-income citizens. These needs and subsequent demands lead to conflict with the political "establishment" but the idea that there is a political and economic system that is structured and acts to support the minority is not part of their orientation. Power of citizens in their view is gained within the fabric of American (or now British or Canadian) democracy and is unproblematic. At the same time, the process of leadership-building and citizen action, although constrained ideologically, is part of the process. The other three groups are oppositional. ACORN does not "name the system" but it is critical about the concentration of wealth and the role of the state in supporting distribution towards the wealthy and corporations. Its orientation is to campaign against this concentration and to make demands that lead to redistribution of wealth towards low- and middle-income people. There are many examples of this approach, including campaigns against predatory lending or campaigns for a living wage. The focus can be described as redistribution through popular campaigns and building power for low- and middle-income people (see Rathke, 2009). However, at the same time, this approach is not anti-capitalist and victories can lead to partnership with corporate bodies to develop programs. Right to the City Alliance has a radical stance and challenges neo-liberal capitalism. In addition, as opposed to both ACORN and IAF, many of the Alliance's member organizations "name the system" and include educational programs so that members and leaders can deepen their analysis. FRAPRU has a clear anti-neo-liberal perspective in its positions and demands strong state intervention as a means of social provision and economic redistribution. This message is carried in its campaigns and member organizations. RTTCA and FRAPRU engage in a strong critique, which helps members develop an analysis of why things are the way they are and attempt to make changes through strong collective action by the working class. There is an inherent tension between the limitations inherent in the structures and functions of the system and the struggles for justice within it. The underlying belief is that winning victories builds power—and yet, with a critical analysis of the nature of the system, it is understood that the victories are not an end in themselves but part of a long march to build a strong movement of opposition and work towards basic social change. The organizations discussed here, despite their differences, are examples of action organizations that work with a conflict model and contest power. They have continued through thirty years of neo-liberal transformation in opposition to both the dominant direction in the wider society and the general tendencies of community organizations, which will be discussed in the next chapter.

# CHAPTER FIVE

# COMMUNITY AS CONTAINMENT OR NEW POSSIBILITIES?

In this chapter I will examine the dominant approaches to community work that emerged as a result of the shifts in social and economic policy that began in the late 1970s and accelerated after the 1980s. The relationship between the state, the market, individuals, and the community were reorganized in this period, shifting responsibilities and obligations, particularly for social provision and service delivery. As a consequence, community that was defined through local organizations played a more important role. These changes were discussed in chapter 2; here, I will look at the resulting practices and their underlying assumptions. In the models discussed earlier, I argued that the dominant approach to development was a consensus-oriented ideology whose goal is to bring diverse actors together to put in place a service or a development process that serves all interests. These would fit into the Integration/Development quadrant according to the table 1.1 in chapter 1. At the same time, there are other approaches that have integrated service provision and alternative development as a strategy of social change, and these would be part of opposition and development. Examples of these will also be provided. Although important, these practices are not the dominant ones and tend to stand outside of mainstream community development. There is also a midpoint between these two approaches. Practitioners and theorists of community development in the post-1980s have argued that the role played by community has progressive possibilities even within the mainstream of practice; and, further, that support from government and private foundations has created opportunities for innovative practice and positive social change. I will present some examples of this approach and its limits. The basic question is this: with community becoming state policy, has the current period created an opportunity for community organizations to play a role in a process of progressive social change? Or has it brought the community into the orbit of state regulation through these organizations—or are both possible at the same time?

Community development has a long history in Canada and elsewhere. Its importance has shifted within the wider political and economic contexts. After playing second fiddle to social action during the relatively short period described in the previous chapter, community development has made a comeback, once again becoming the dominant form of practice. I will begin here with a brief historical perspective and definitions of this approach.

Jim Lotz (1998) has traced the history of community development, providing examples such as land grant colleges in the United States that aimed to improve living conditions of rural communities in the early twentieth century, as well as attempts by French-speaking minorities in Nova Scotia to create cultural and economic institutions that would preserve their linguistic and cultural heritage. In addition, he discusses the role of community development in managing the British Empire in the 1930s. Rothman (1974) cites a definition of community development from a United Nations document written in 1955. This definition is a useful description and includes the practice's central elements. It states:

> Community development can be tentatively defined as a
> process designed to create conditions of economic and social
> progress for the whole community with its active participation
> and the fullest reliance on the community's initiative. (United
> Nations Secretary General, 1955, p. 6)

Some of the dominant values include "democratic procedures, voluntary cooperation, self-help, development of indigenous leadership and education" (p. 4). Similarly, at a 1954 conference in Cambridge, UK, community development was defined as "a movement designed to promote better living for the whole community with the active participation and on the initiative of the whole community" (Lotz, 1998, p. 119). Lotz describes community development workers as "an odd blend of idealists and realists, seeking better ways of meeting human needs than the societies offered the ordinary people of their time" (p. 125). Elsewhere he writes that community workers would encourage "cooperation between all residents" and "self-help and local enterprise" (Lotz, 1997, p. 25). Lotz cites Lagassé, a Metis social worker, who describes his own beliefs as follows:

1. That all people, no matter how unambitious they may appear, have a desire to better themselves.
2. The difficulties preventing the fulfillment of people's needs are too great for the resources, that they have.
3. All groups can do something to help themselves when given an opportunity to do so on their own terms.
4. In order to achieve lasting change it is necessary to influence simultaneously human behavior. (Lagassé cited in Lotz, 1997, p. 23)

Similar perspectives reappear in the 1990s (see, for example, Kretzman and McKnight, 1993; Homan, 1999; and Ewalt et al., 1998). Frank and Smith (1999) propose the following definition of community development:

> Community development is the planned evolution of all aspects of community well-being (economic, social, environmental and cultural). It is a process whereby community members come together to take collective action and generate solutions to common problems.... The primary outcome of community development is improved quality of life. Effective community development results in mutual benefits and responsibility among community members. (p. 6)

Although there is a rhetoric of change, in contrast to the social or community action approach, this change is usually focused inward on the community itself rather than outward on the wider social, economic, and political structures. Further, the process of working towards these changes is through consensus-building across interests rather than organizing to promote specific interests of the poor or oppressed groups. The emphasis is on meeting needs and finding pragmatic ways to do so that do not challenge those with power. There is little discussion about inequality, interest, power, or the ways that development can challenge these factors that play such a large role in shaping the social issues and problems. Lotz (1998) raises questions about the role and impact of community development, observing that, "in a paradoxical way, community development strives to stabilize society and encourage innovation and change in human relationships" (p. 26). This perspective stands in clear contrast to the action approach, which begins with an analysis of power and how it operates and promotes organizing as a tool for those without power to strengthen their collective voices. Community development believes in the democratic participation of people in finding solutions to issues and problems, but this occurs within boundaries shaped by the power relations already in place. It offers opportunities for building democratic practices and creating ways that people can learn to take greater control of their own lives. However, the dominant practice in this period reinforces the overriding power relations rather than challenging them.

In analyzing the shift in community practice, the context has to be taken into account as an important factor. As discussed in chapter 2, the context for community practice has been altered since the 1980s with the shift in who holds responsibility for social provision—from the welfare state to a combination of the market (privatization), the family, and organizations in local communities. "Community as social policy" became coincident with the rise of globalization, economic restructuring, and the cutbacks of the welfare state. The community sector, promoted by the state and other social actors, acted in response to the consequences of this restructuring. With the state provision on the decline, the ascent of community becomes a feature of the new approach to social provision. How does this shift express itself? To answer this, we must consider theoretical perspectives along with concepts such as rebuilding civil society and social capital, asset-based community development, comprehensive community initiatives, and consensus organizing, which have become the new buzzwords in the theories that shape community practice.

## REBUILDING CIVIL SOCIETY AND SOCIAL CAPITAL

Social capital and rebuilding civil society are two concepts that, after the 1980s, were widely adopted as theoretical perspectives with important implications for community development. Given the extensive debates and literature around both of these concepts, I shall present brief definitions of each and then raise questions about how these concepts have shaped the development model. Homan (1999) states that

> Social capital refers to community wealth derived from active engagement of individuals with other members of the community. ... These engagements provide opportunities for affiliation among members and benefits to the community. (p. 31)

Clarke and Gaile (1998) argue that social as well as human capital provide important resources that contribute towards national economic competitiveness and the restructuring of local citizenship. In order for cities, for example, to be able to achieve economic success, both human capital (i.e., an educated workforce) and social capital (i.e., a local infrastructure) are necessary. However, despite the good reasons for having resources tied to social capital, some writers have been concerned about the difficulty in creating and sustaining it. This position is put forward in Putnam's (1995) important article, "Bowling Alone: America's Declining Social Capital." He offers many reasons for this decline, including the entry of women into the labour market, the decline of the trade union movement, and the growth of privatized forms of entertainment. McKnight (1995) joins in this chorus and attributes the reduction of social capital to the dominant role played by professionals in many aspects of social life. So there is a problem; social capital is necessary to enhance daily life, yet it is declining and difficult to re-establish. Putnam (1995) concludes that the public agenda should add "the question of how to reverse these adverse trends in social connectedness, thus restoring civic engagement and civic trust" (p. 77). With the retreat of government and the fragmentation of neighbourhoods as social units, the renewal of community development begins to surface as a strategy that can restore local social practices to fill these voids. At the same time, this practice does not challenge the underlying causes of these problems.

In the 1980s, civil society was promoted as a strategy to counter the shift away from state provision and related cutbacks. The Caledon Institute is a leading promoter in Canada of community development as a means of poverty alleviation and social development. Torjman's (1997) essay, entitled *Civil Society: Reclaiming Our Humanity*, illustrates this position. It promotes the growth of civil society to achieve three major objectives: "caring communities, economic security, and ... promot[ing] social investment ... [with] resources include[ing] public dollars, encourages partnerships and collaborative working arrangements, addresses issues in a holistic and integrated way" (p. 2). All sectors including governments, business, labour, education, foundations, and social agencies must take responsibility for tackling economic, social, and environmental issues. Active citizenship implies building caring communities that embody both rights and responsibilities.

The following ingredients are the basis for a civil society. The first is capital—and this includes finance, natural/built, and human capital. Finance capital is defined as a range of practices from community loan funds where control of capital is in the hands of community-based organizations, credit unions which support micro-business, and private sector corporations and/or foundations that support some types of community initiatives. Natural/built capital refers to the use of space, including land and buildings. The range here is wide, and it includes community ownership strategies such as land trusts and the use of facilities such as shopping malls. Human capital is defined as "the wealth inherent in human resources" (Torjman, 1997, p. 11), based on the capacities of all to contribute and the mobilization of these capacities through voluntary efforts.

Partnerships are the second ingredient and are defined as "strategic alliances between business and non-profit groups for the purpose of promoting economic and social well-being" (Torjman, 1997, p. 12). Different types of partnerships are presented including social marketing, employee volunteerism, and direct involvement in social and economic change. Partnerships are deemed important because they raise awareness of social problems and create more resources. At the same time, the document argues that partnership complements and supplements the public sector, and embodies the message that economic, social, and environmental issues are the concerns of the whole community. The call for a renewal of civil society is shaped by the need to reconstruct community as a place of service and support, a place in which all interests can come together for everyone's benefit.

There are common elements of the promotion of civil society, social capital, and community development. The ideas and practices are based on an assumption that society is shaped by the common concern of all rather than conflicts of interest, and that social and economic partnerships are the means to put this practice in place. Because these are key elements, I would like to raise a couple of critical issues on the topics of interest and partnership. It is these issues that differentiate community action from the development models. The analysis presented in the Caledon document and the other ideas cited above imply that all members of society share a common stake and responsibility. This position is politically dangerous because it overlooks questions of interest and power. Citizens, corporations, and government have never shared common interests. To announce a new "caring, mutually responsible society" is to wipe the historical slate clean, despite the fact that underlying interests remain. Similarly, to start with the categories of "individual" and "citizen" assumes a commonality which history has never delivered. We need to begin the discussion with class, gender, race, and location on the globe, and then examine how social life is defined by interest. The historical discontinuity of the above positions is coupled with a political naïveté. The implicit prescription is a common interest—that all of us want to walk into the "promised land," hand in hand. This remedy to the problems created by the current economic and social process of redefinition is a recipe for a social disaster as it implies the dismantling of opposition for a consensus, which overrides interest.

The argument that all sectors must take responsibility is fine in the most general terms, but we know historically that it is precisely because capital and the state did not assume their responsibilities for social provision that there have been and continue to be social struggles aimed at extracting social gains. Why were these struggles necessary? First and foremost this is because capital—first locally, then nationally, and now globally—is not self-regulating, and the only way that capital became regulated was through state intervention to limit its power through legislation, such as minimum wage and welfare state programs. There has never been anything approaching "equal responsibility"; capital has no vested interest in place or people. It is a relation in which those who control it can and will do what they have to do in order to push for profit. At best, the approach described above will be tinkering with the consequences of economic restructuring and state cutbacks through the provision of unstable local services and a few programs. Our efforts have to focus on the root of the problems and the alliances necessary to challenge their underlying power relations.

One of the common assumptions of the new community developers is that partnerships between different groups in the society are an inherent part of social change. Many issues arise from this position. First, partnerships are real when they are established between different groups within a common project in which the goals and values are clearly defined and shared. This implies a process of discussion and debate between partners and a consensus between movements on all sides. This is quite different than a partnership in which one group—such as the corporate sector, to use the examples cited in the Caledon document—drops in and does something for or with the community sector. The former implies a common project that shares power among the different participants, while the latter is an extension of a charity relation under a different label.

The question, however, is what kinds of compromises are made by the community sector when entering into partnerships with socially and economically stronger partners. This brings us back to the earlier discussion on the issues of power and interest. Why is it that the corporate sector is willing to enter into partnerships when it comes to social intervention, but does not ask the community sector to join into partnerships when it comes to questions of corporate policy? For example, corporations make policies all the time that have major impacts on the local community, such as downsizing or shifting investment elsewhere; where are community organizations in these processes? The community sector can organize food banks for the unemployed, and maybe receive some corporate donations to do that, but where is the real public accountability of those entities that are motivated by private profit? Until this happens, the partnership relationship will be skewed to one side with the community sector as a very small player. Partnerships are the current currency of community development. They pull community organizations into relationships that hide power and interest.

The promotion of these definitions of civil society and social/human capital as a direction for the community movement raises a number of difficulties. Their position obscures a basic assumption: in order to contribute to the process of social change, community organizations have to understand society from the viewpoint of their interests. The use of civil society and human/social capital, from the mainstream point of view, obscures the specific interests of groups such as the poor, women, and many minorities. These groups face barriers not because of who they are but because of social policies and processes. The demands and struggles for social justice must be the central agenda for community organizations. This is the starting point. Having argued this, can notions of civil society be useful? In the context of protest against the international organizations promoting freer trade and greater corporate power, the term "civil society organizations" has been used to refer to the wide range of popular non-governmental organizations (NGOs) involved in the opposition. The use of this term is loose and as such is too inclusive; it lacks a conceptual framework. However, it points to the large number of groups and organizations that do exist and at times mobilize together in opposition. The concept of "civil society" needs to be considered as contradictory, describing the wide range of organizations that position themselves in opposing ways. Some actively participate in a new social consensus and work towards responses to deteriorating social and economic conditions that do not challenge those with power, while others are active in their opposition to the prevailing economic and social arrangements. Some organizations can live in both places, providing new services and then mobilizing for demonstrations. Jamie Swift (1999) captures this tension within civil society:

> The concerns of civil society ... are clearly not the concerns
> of unfettered market forces that generate social disintegration
> and inequality. This thing called civil society, then, has a role
> in the protection of the public good, even if, again, it cannot
> automatically be assumed to be a Good Thing ... or looked on
> as a neo-liberal substitute for the state.... These projects [services] are fine, but do little by themselves to enable people ...
> to take more control over the decisions that have an impact
> on their lives.... we can locate civil society as a space, separate
> from formal politics but very much politically engaged, where
> people act on issues that impinge on them directly or where
> they promote a more general public good. (p. 147)

Thus, we see how there is a dual meaning and possibility. Civil society is described as a space that is neither occupied by the economy nor the state, yet is not necessarily independent of them. Within this space a variety of activities is possible, ranging from protest to very conventional charities. At the same time, the building of civil society has been promoted and supported as a way to replace state services and build a stifling social consensus and partnership. Knowing the difference is the beginning of a politics of social change.

## ASSET-BASED COMMUNITY DEVELOPMENT

A major proponent of the renewal of community development is John McKnight. He has written extensively and consulted widely with a large variety of organizations and people who have power to influence community practice, such as the foundations that support these activities. His work is complex and combines both a radical and a conservative vision. His radicalism comes in the form of a fundamental challenge to the power of professionals, particularly those who work in the community— for example, social workers and a wide variety of the so-called helping professions. He defines one of the most significant problems facing the United States to be the growing control of all aspects of daily life by those professions, which as a consequence have eclipsed the democratic life of the community. He writes,

> It is clear that the economic pressure to professionalize requires an expanding universe of need and the magnification of deficiency. This form of marginal professional development can only intensify the ineffective, dominating, and iatrogenic nature of the professional class as they invade the remaining perimeters of personhood. (McKnight, 1995, pp. 23–4)

His task is to find a way to "dissolve the 'professional problem'" (p. 25). From there he constructs a perspective that is based on citizenship (as opposed to clients) and assets (as opposed to deficiencies). He argues for a practice that strengthens the capacity of people to control and manage their lives through a vibrant and democratic community. This argument is developed in McKnight's more recent work in collaboration with Block (2010). They extend their critique from the "professional problem" to a critique of consumer society, converting citizens into consumers with two costs: the undermining of family functions and the isolation of people from communities. For the purposes of this discussion, it is the loss of community and the resulting reduction in what they call community competency that is important. As a consequence, institutions play a greater role, encourage dependency, and reduce the power of local communities. This causes neighbourhoods to lose in two ways: the institutions cannot deliver and community skills become weakened. The program of change grows out of the community/neighbourhood by re-appropriating power and building a role in social provision and economic development through two sources of power: "the expression of our gifts and their manifestation through our association with our neighbors" (p. 109). They present a vision of a decentralized society of communities that plays a primary role based on mutual aid and volunteerism.

In practice, Kretzmann and McKnight (1993) argue that the solution cannot be found by focusing on deficiencies and problems, which is the way that these issues are usually approached. These types of intervention usually command most of an organization's resources. They counter with a different starting point: a clear commitment to a community's capacities and assets. The traditional practice is to point out problems and then to construct services as a solution to them, which then creates a dependency and reduces people from their potential status as citizens to clients with a reliance on outside experts. This "needs-based strategy can guarantee only survival and can never lead to serious change or community development … this orientation must be replaced as one of the major causes of the sense of hopelessness that pervades discussion about the future of low-income communities" (Kretzmann and McKnight, 1993, p. 5). They propose an alternative that they call "capacity-focused development." Their position has two central ideas. First, significant community development can only take place when local people commit themselves to investing their resources and efforts, thus avoiding a top-down or an outside-in practice. Second, the prospect for outside help is bleak because of budgetary constraints and weak job prospects. The basic goal is to mobilize assets in order to build community by involving "virtually the entire community in the complex process of regeneration" (p. 345). The basic solution to the professional service problem is to use existing assets pulled together within the community to create networks of self-help and support. They believe that "identifying the variety and richness of skills, talents, knowledge of people in low-income neighborhoods provides a base upon which to build new approaches and enterprises" (cited in Minkler and Wallerstein, 1999 p. 160). However, they recognize some of the limits of what can be achieved locally and argue that low-income neighbourhoods should "develop their assets and become interdependent with mainstream people, groups and economic activity" (p. 171).

The disciples of McKnight disregard the "professional problem" and consumerism. Instead, they pull out those parts that fit nicely into an acceptable practice for neo-liberalism and then professionalize them. For example, Homan (1999) presents a summary of the elements of practice that follow from this perspective. The starting point is the recognition that the existing assets of a community are those factors that give it the energy to take action. Teaching individuals a variety of skills builds on their capacities. Connecting people and building relationships allows individuals to share their talents through linkages with existing community resources. He states, "Whenever you connect resources, you create investors.... You extend ownership and participation" (p. 37). The next step in the process is to create or increase community resources—to bring something new into existence. A pillar of this process is community ownership of its direction, actions, and resources—in other words, allowing the community to create the plans, not just approve them. An expectation is that the members of the community will do all the work if possible. Simultaneously with building on internal capacity, beneficial external relations are necessary with allies, other communities, and additional sources of public support. The fundamental goal is to foster community self-reliance and confidence. This can be achieved through self-sustaining organizations, effective mechanisms for community decision-making, and a renewal of leadership. These steps are intended to enhance the community's general quality of life. The question of who will support these initiatives and provide the resources for them is ignored, including the dicey relationship between local organizations and those who fund them.

This approach builds on the older traditions of community development that emphasize process and participation of citizens, and it insists on local control of community processes with citizens playing an active role in building community projects. However, this is not new. It has always been at the core of community organizing. The idea of people having power to control local institutions and processes is a necessary first step, but a step towards what? This question is at the heart of the differences between community/social action and development. McKnight (1995) clarifies this difference by arguing that

> Organizations originally oriented to the goal of equalizing consumption patterns between and within neighborhoods are increasingly turning toward an agenda that centers on building internal neighborhood productive capacities. (p. 157)

In other words, do not look outside for help, for redistribution of wealth and income, but fulfil your own needs by mobilizing local resources. There is an echo here from earlier times. It is the "bootstrap" theory of poverty reduction. According to this theory, if the poor worked hard and prepared themselves adequately, then they too could succeed within capitalist society. Thus, the critique of this approach is that it focuses on changing internal community processes but ignores the underlying assumptions about why this should be done and the subsequent political agenda that it implicitly supports. We can understand this when we fit McKnight's position into the wider social and economic context, particularly the changing role and ideology of the state.

McKnight's approach gained importance in the mid-1980s. That particular context certainly contributed to the acceptance of community development as part of the mainstream by governments, foundations, and those in practice, as well as researchers and writers in the field. The changes of context are important in understanding the emergence of new forms and ideas of practice. The period from the late 1970s brought rapid and substantial changes in economic and political life. One of the consequences, for example, was that rather than attacking poverty, governments launched offensives against the poor and other marginal populations themselves, not only by removing programs and benefits but also by assailing the basic entitlements to these programs. Economic changes paralleled the redefinition of the state's role. Unions were put on the defensive as employers sought a more "flexible" workplace to enable greater competition in global markets. This push and accelerating technological innovation brought massive unemployment in the 1980s and much of the 1990s. The new jobs that replaced traditional blue-collar work were neither unionized nor stable. In both Canada and the USA, poverty was not diminished because, for many, work became more precarious and irregular. Further, we have entered a world of global capitalism in which markets rule, and the bottom line is on top. There is a deeply rooted feeling that the possibilities of progressive social change no longer exist, and there seems to be little for those with a progressive social vision. The traditional social democratic parties and the Democratic Party in the USA have all abandoned their social commitments and supported the corporate agenda. The turn to local volunteerism advocated by McKnight and his colleagues is limited to say the least, and in reality it does not challenge the growing concentration of wealth and income, nor the growing inequalities. Without redistribution, even if communities had the capacity to take on the functions envisioned by this approach, they would not have the resources, which short of robbing banks can only be provided by state programs.

In order to understand how ideas such as asset-building gained so much credibility, we can examine the response of some community organizing practice to the transformation of the wider economic and social changes linked to neo-liberalism. At first, activists in the community sector opposed the cutbacks in government spending on services and programs. As the years passed, it became clear that neo-liberalism was gaining rather than losing ground and, as the new economy emerged from the restructuring, it appeared that a return to the post-war employment patterns and the welfare state was unlikely. Community organizations and organizers faced a dismal situation. There did not seem to be the energy to continue the types of social action struggles of the 1960s and the 1970s, and the situation of poverty and unemployment, coupled with a reduction in social programs, drove large numbers of new clients to community-based organizations and services for help. The community sector responded with social solidarity, provided new forms of social support, and created ways to build local solidarity; however, these strategies lost their political edge. One example of this is programs like food banks, which became a growth industry in the 1980s and a permanent part of the landscape by the 1990s.

Pushed by the new realities, the community organizations looked for wider strategies to combat the social and economic problems that they faced. The "shift" that McKnight and Kretzmann discussed above describes the repositioning of community organizations from an oppositional to a collaborative stance, from seeking confrontation and challenging the power structure to finding common ground and building a new social consensus with it. Further, both governments and private foundations have embraced this new community development practice. These bodies have subsequently supported many of the new initiatives that use this approach. Part of the reason for this is that community organizations have cushioned the blows to the poor and the working class that resulted from the changes described above. At the same time, these organizations have tried to go beyond service provision to promote local revitalization strategies while asking for very little from the state.

Criticisms have been raised in relation to McKnight and the related community development practices. McGrath, Moffat, and George (1999) raise four issues. First, the discussion of community capacity-building is ahistorical and ignores the many rich traditions that have gone before it, such as popular education and feminism. The assumptions that McKnight uses on the necessity of building local capacity are not new; they have been used before, often with a vision of fundamental social change. Second, the approach assumes that there is unused capacity within communities that can be released by a community development process. McGrath et al. argue that this position assumes the availability of voluntary labour as the basis for this capacity. Further, the growth of women's employment in wage labour and the demands on care-giving because of state cutbacks of services diminishes their contribution, even if that kind of volunteer activity were desirable. Thus, the model may be more applicable for wealthier communities. Third, as opposed to McKnight who, they say, assumes a coherence in local communities, these authors state that communities are fragmented by identity and interest, arguing that one cannot necessarily find either unity or common ties within them. Finally, they challenge McKnight's belief that the community sector is independent of the state. In contrast, they point out how the organizations and processes have been shaped by the changes in the welfare state, both through funding and the definition of their activities. These issues get at some of the limits of the new community development practices and approaches.

Another problem associated with an increased emphasis on the community development model is that the local community has very limited power to shape its internal processes. In contrast, David Morris (1996) has a different understanding of local power. He promotes the idea that "authority, responsibility, and capacity are the cornerstones of sustainable communities" (p. 437). Authority implies the mandate to make rules that protect and enhance community life. As opposed to the conservatives, who support responsibility and capacity, the notion of authority raises the dimension of decentralized power that can be used formally by those at the local level to effect real change by having control over economic processes. Decision-making over zoning or economic planning is an example of the type of questions that residents should control. Capacity-building without political power is dead-ended. In addition, for Morris, capacity implies the power and confidence that comes with ownership of economic tools. As he states:

> Authority, responsibility, capacity: the ARC of community. Without authority, democracy is meaningless. Without responsibility, chaos ensues. Without productive capacity, we are helpless to manage our affairs and determine our economic future. (Morris, 1996, p. 445)

Thus, the concept of capacity-building and the related process of community development in and of themselves are not the problem, but it is the context in which they are practised that is key. If the push is to use these processes to build local power and authority, to mobilize low-income populations, and to struggle for social justice, then they can contribute to a social change strategy. If the goal is to make limited changes in community life as an end in itself and as a way of creating networks of "helpful citizens," then the outcome will support the neo-liberal policies we have seen imposed in recent years.

## CANADIAN EXAMPLE: VIBRANT COMMUNITIES

Comprehensive Community Initiatives (CCI) provides another example of the new community development. It has been adopted as an influential approach across Canada; it has been supported intellectually and promoted by the Caledon and Tamarack Institutes; and it is funded (although not exclusively) by the McConnell Foundation, one of the largest foundations in Canada. Staying within the framework that solutions to problems can be found locally, Ewalt (1998) argues that CCI is an example of a "multifaceted approach that addresses the physical and economic conditions of a neighborhood as well as the social and cultural aspects" (p. 3). These initiatives are based on community partnership or some form of local governance with citizen participation in decision-making. Naparstek and Dooley (1998) discuss a community-building approach that

> looks at the whole picture, acknowledges the interconnectedness of people- and place-based strategies, and recommends a course of action in which solutions are tied together in such a way that they reinforce one another.... that will give neighborhood residents more control over changes and the ability to hold accountable the larger systems that ought to be serving them. (p. 11)

This approach originated when the federal government in the United States created the Empowerment Zone program in 1993, which was designed to support neighbourhood development and alleviate poverty. The program has four elements: a geographically defined target, strategic planning based on a definition of community, community participation in the governance of these programs, and comprehensive development—economic, physical, and human (Chaskin, Joseph, and Chipenda-Dansokho, 1998). The push for a focus on the local comes from a context in which the wider social programs that might have had a major impact—such as wide-scale construction of social housing, adequate income support, federal health care, or initiatives to regulate economic development—have disappeared from national agendas. In their place, the community is given the responsibility to revitalize the local with programs that are administered locally and yet controlled from the outside. The internal processes of community development thus become vehicles for the implementation of a "de-responsiblized" national government, and through local democratic processes they act, perhaps unintentionally, to legitimate these changes.

Vibrant Communities is perhaps the largest and most comprehensive community development initiative in Canada. It draws on the ideas discussed above, and it prioritizes the goal of poverty reduction. Its practices are documented in a recent book edited by Mark Cabaj (2011). Several of its principles integrate the post-1980s community development framework. They argue that, for poverty reduction to be effective, leadership should be multi-sectoral and the collaboration to lead the initiative should include business, government, non-profit groups, and the poor themselves. In addition, effectiveness comes from building on local assets as opposed to looking for solutions outside the community (Cabaj, 2011, p. 7). These principles draw upon the notion of consensus and local assets as promoted by McKnight. The debate with this approach centres around how much of poverty is locally caused versus how much is rooted in the structure and processes of capitalist economies and the current neo-liberal policies of government that have cut social programs and helped to concentrate wealth through changes in taxation. And, along the same line, how many resources do local communities have to actually make a difference—are they capable of securing decent housing and income and regulating labour conditions? My own position should be clear in the way these questions are phrased. Poverty is deeply rooted within the capitalist economy and it is in the interests of employers to keep wages low—and for the state to make it more desirable to work as opposed to staying home and receiving income support programs. Those with a direct stake in changing the situation should be leading the fight against these conditions—low-wage workers, women, and allies within the wider working class. In addition, if poverty is to be reduced, substantial state intervention is required, such as better income support programs and improved minimum wages and labour conditions. This cannot happen at the local level, except by building organizations that will fight for these changes. As I argued with DeFilippis and Fisher (DeFilippis, Fisher, and Shragge, 2010),

> community efforts need to understand their work as transcending the community. We see the political potential from community emerging when there is an emphasis on working 'within a place,' rather than 'about a place.' ... community-based efforts must address and confront issues and problems

within a community *and* create linkages beyond the local (pp. 168–9).

Despite the flawed and limited perspectives of this approach, there has been some interesting practice that has both integrative and oppositional opportunities.

One of Vibrant Community's supported projects is Vivre Saint-Michel en santé (VSMS). In many ways, the emergence of this organization was an example of the evolution of community organizations in Quebec. Saint-Michel was founded as an independent municipality and had a strong industrial base that grew rapidly in the late 1940s and 1950s. Like many neighbourhoods in Montreal, in the period after 1960 there was a decline in Saint-Michel's industrial base and a referendum in 1968 brought it into the City of Montreal. Currently, the district is a multicultural one with many new immigrants, and it faces a range of challenges linked to poverty and economic decline (Toye, 2011). Community organizing began there in the 1970s with a popular citizens' organization that gradually evolved into a community "table de concertation." The current organization was initiated in the context of the district's continuing deterioration. In 1991, 200 citizens and representatives of community organizations met under the theme of "Rendez-vous de la dernière chance" (last chance meeting) and set up the table de concertation Vivre St-Michel en santé (Renaud, 2008). The wider community sector was also in a process of transition at the same time, forming local tables (partnerships) with representation from the private, public, and community sectors on themes of local revitalization and economic development. In addition, funding became available from the city and from Centraide (United Way) for these new structures. Persistent poverty was a source of frustration to VSMS and they embarked on a process of strategic planning, commissioning a private sector consultant. By 2003, they had become a member of Vibrant Communities, and they developed priorities and strategies to reduce poverty through local work. The four main areas of intervention were: training and employment; adequate, affordable housing; improved services for culture, sports, and in the commercial sector; and improved urban security (Toye, 2011). The organization has worked to strengthen processes for citizen participation, leadership development, and obtaining concrete outcomes. Toye (2011) summarizes what he describes as its impressive achievements. By 2010, for example, VSMS had worked with employers to hire 900 neighbourhood residents, and through their efforts in partnership with developers 170 units of affordable housing were created, cultural activities were established, local artists were supported, an urban security plan was developed with police and municipal officials, and recreation facilities are currently being planned. The work of VSMS was able to bring about some important gains in the local community. Whether it affects poverty or reduces it is another question. Services can improve the lives of low-income people but the relations of power and the interests served by these relations do not seem to change.

In commenting on strategy, Toye (2011) observes that "collaborating with government is a less familiar strategy than mobilizing, opposing governmental decisions, and confronting government for positive change" (p. 59). This is the core of the debate. VSMS is a complex organization that requires professional leadership and management. The structure with government representation allows a process of negotiation, but what is the role of residents in this process and how much power do they have? Also, what are the limits of the politics of social change? In contrasting VSMS to organizations discussed at the end of chapter 4, we see some clear differences. VSMS is a professional and state-shaped organization; citizen participation is mobilized periodically in assemblies or through representatives and within pre-existing programmatic parameters. In contrast, FRAPRU, for example, sees organizing and mobilizing citizens as its basis of power and legitimacy. Its autonomy from the state widens its criticism, and its potential as an oppositional body that can work to change the direction of its society. Organizations like VSMS and the others in Vibrant Communities are able to achieve some positive gains, mainly services, without challenging the relations of domination and power that keep the system working in the interests served by neo-liberal capitalism.

## COMMUNITY ECONOMIC DEVELOPMENT (CED) AND THE SOCIAL ECONOMY

Community organizers adopted CED as a strategy in the late 1980s, primarily but not exclusively in response to the deterioration of local economies and the lack of hope for revitalization from the outside—either from the private market through investment or with the support of government programs. Initiatives with leadership from community organizations and partnerships with local actors were designed to create new economic options that would provide jobs, services, or infrastructure. The partnerships included representatives from the private sector, unions, local institutions, and government. Through these processes, community organizations became players in the process of economic development (Shragge, 1997). The practices that they use have varied—from the promotion of small-scale enterprises that were put in place to employ people who faced long-term unemployment, to loan funds to support CED initiatives, to planning initiatives that promoted local economic development. The underlying goals were to find ways to revitalize local economies, ameliorate poverty through training and job creation, and to involve residents and other local actors in these processes.

Social solidarity, as well as the recognition that the state had abandoned its responsibility and was unlikely to resume its role as the central provider, motivated the emphasis on economic development and related services. Further, a new strategy of consensus-based partnerships created alliances of community organizations, businesses, government, and, at times, unions (particularly in Quebec) to sponsor these local initiatives, which aimed to find limited solutions to problems without examining their causes. These partnerships obscured conflicting interests and differentials in power. The community sector, as the politically weakest player, did the front-line work of implementing programs defined from the outside by government and foundations. The trouble, then, was how local organizations could maintain enough autonomy to define and put in place activities that reflected neighbourhood priorities. The resulting differences between organizations and government reflected the strength of local groups, their traditions, and their own approaches to CED practice. As CED evolved it became known as the social economy. The practices are similar, but the difference, as the definitions below will demonstrate, is that CED has a geographic-neighbourhood framework, and its intervention is framed by its relationship to place-based development. The social economy is focused on socially oriented business development, and it does not have a comprehensive community vision.

I became involved in CED in the mid-1980s. A private foundation had supported an initiative to bring local organizations together in a

Montreal district to explore whether or not CED could improve conditions of low-income people. My role was to write an evaluation of the grant. More importantly, I had questions about the limits and possibilities of solving poverty through local work. These questions are still the most important ones. What role can CED and the social economy play in the processes of social change? Would CED act to reproduce capitalist forms of development, or would it be an opportunity to create new forms and approaches and to democratize economic development? Definitions of CED reflect underlying contested analyses and values. Swack (1992) argues that the premise of CED is the strengthening of local capacity to mobilize resources and build a strong economic base for the community. CED seeks to change the economic structure of the community and build permanent economic institutions, thus implying greater control of local resources. CED is a people-initiated strategy that seeks to develop the economy of the community, region, or country for the benefit of its residents. It is a systematic and planned intervention that is intended to promote economic self-reliance. A principal objective of CED is to help consumers in becoming producers, users in becoming providers, and employees in becoming owners of enterprises. CED does not assume that the market alone will solve the economic problems of communities. It utilizes entrepreneurship methods similar to those used by traditional businesses in the private sector to develop efficient, productive, and profitable ventures and enterprises, but does so in the context of a community's social, cultural, and political values. Swack's definition is fundamental and looks at the potential of local initiatives to use economic development as a tool to achieve social ends.

Not all CED perspectives are based on the same premises. Fontan (1993) differentiates between "liberal" and "progressive" CED. The liberal tradition is economic development for and by the community. It does not challenge basic economic relations but it employs business development from the bottom up. It aims to repair the economic fabric of the private sector in order to create jobs. Local revitalization can take place through the promotion of private entrepreneurship and related measures to develop the "employability" of the population and the creation of related jobs. In contrast, the progressive vision is broader and places greater emphasis on social processes. Thus the progressive tradition attempts to integrate economic and social development; improve the community's environment and quality of services; build local control over ownership; and create alternative, non-traditional economic forms such as cooperatives, alternative businesses, community enterprises, self-managed organizations, and non-profits.

Bruyn (1987) and Roseland (1998) have developed progressive orientations. Bruyn argues that, historically, we have been presented a false choice between a free market with electoral democracy versus an undemocratic, restrictive, interventionist state-centred planning (state socialism). He argues for a third option in which the role of the state is not to regulate the economy but to enable it to regulate itself and become accountable to the people it affects. In order to overcome the problem of the market destroying the community without government control, the social emancipation of land, labour, and capital from the competitive market is a required step. It is a process leading to local autonomy. He argues that this transition can take place within the context of economic viability at the local level. Bruyn and his colleagues, in a volume titled *Beyond the State and the Market* (Bruyn and Meehan, 1987), demonstrate the viability of this strategy of transformation. They cite examples of how land, labour, and capital have been reinvented through local action. For example, community land trusts are a way of creating local ownership of land and keeping it out of the market. Worker cooperatives have a long tradition and are a tool that labour can use to own the means of production. Finally, there are examples of community loan associations or credit unions through which capital can be democratically managed for local use. These are examples of alternatives created within the existing system that use economic tools for social objectives within a democratic framework.

Roseland (1998) provides a perspective that merges the principles and goals of CED and green businesses in order to move towards what he calls "sustainable communities" (p. 160). Self-reliance implies that the community enhances its wealth through the development of it resources. Tools to achieve this include maximizing the use of existing resources, circulating money within the community, reducing imports of goods and services, and creating new products. He also emphasizes the use of incentives to attract environmentally responsible businesses. Roseland argues that self-reliance does not imply that absence of support from outside bodies, including the government, and he advocates the use of lobbying for policies that can support the institutions and conditions for this green CED vision. This last point is particularly important because it raises a political dimension and the necessity of outside support in creating the conditions that support local work.

These definitions offer a progressive view and present CED as a strategy of creating democratic forms of economic and social development that works in the interest of the majority and can be sustainable in environmental terms. In practice, the results are more traditional, and CED and the social economy have been an innovative tool to address a variety of needs through professionally led organizations. Toye and Charland's (2006) overview of CED and the social economy in Canada confirm this argument. They summarize this portrait as follows:

> there are a relatively small number of organizations … that can be said to be doing comprehensive, long-term planning for social and economic renewal of an entire geographic community. More common are efforts which are limited to a community of interest or a population within a community and focus on certain aspects of social and economic renewal. (p. 36)

The main areas of activity include "human capital"—for example, training for the labour markets, providing support for small or socially oriented businesses or co-ops, and building community capacity. They suggest that one of the reasons for these directions is that government funding programs lead the development of priorities.

Some CED practice is highly institutionalized through para-governmental organizations. In Montreal, after beginning as local initiatives in working-class neighbourhoods during the mid-1980s, coalitions of labour, community organizations, and businesses sought strategies to combat poverty and unemployment that was a result of economic deterioration and factory closures. Revitalization strategies were to be put in place through local organizations. These included strategies to either save, restructure, or create new local businesses, and to put training programs in place to get people back into employment. In addition, the structures of these organizations were to involve the local population through representation of different sectors on their boards. After the development of three of these organizations, joint efforts by the municipal, provincial, and federal governments resulted in the establishment of CED organizations in each of the city's administrative districts, with the exception of the downtown core. The programs of these organizations are designed to provide technical and financial support to both traditional and community businesses. They also provide programs designed to enhance local residents' entry into the labour market. With subsequent reforms in the late 1990s these organizations have been integrated into the provincial government network of development agencies. With each reform the autonomy of the organizations has been diminished and their programs narrowed. There is still some opportunity for innovation and support for socially oriented community initiatives, such as daycare, services for the elderly, and projects such as eco-tourism (Fontan et al., 2006). The advantages of these highly institutionalized CED organizations are their stability and the resources that they offer, both technical and financial. The disadvantage is that they have come under the control of the provincial government, and thus the local population has less power to shape the priorities and direction of these organizations. In addition, as they have become part of the mainstream, their activities have begun to focus much more on traditional, market-oriented business development—usually small enterprises, with some social economy projects. The explicitly social aspects have become less pronounced. An important struggle within these organizations has been to use their staff and other resources to provide assistance in finding innovative solutions that go beyond the liberal perspective.

In contrast to institutionalized CED, there are organizations that I would describe as independent that use a CED strategy to reach social ends. Chic Resto-Pop, described in chapter 2, is an example. Another example is A-Way Express in Toronto (see Church, 1997). This business grew out of a movement of people who have endured the mental health system and call themselves psychiatric survivors. It is a courier service whose employees use public transportation to deliver their letters and so on. However, despite its success as a business, it is far more than that. A-Way describes itself as an alternative business. It was established partially to counter the myth that people who have been institutionalized can never work, and to build a community of solidarity for this group. It provides a flexible work environment in which people can negotiate their hours based on their specific needs and capacities. In addition, it is democratically structured with the board of directors drawn mostly from employees. The leadership and the majority of the board are psychiatric survivors. At the same time as A-Way is using a business to reach social ends, it has resisted the idea that the business has to be "self-sustaining." It has successfully negotiated support from different outside bodies on a regular and ongoing basis. This support is justified on the social and health outcomes of the business. Just as the private sector receives many different subsidies, grants, and supports from the government (often the bigger the business, the bigger the support), it is an error to assume that CED initiatives must sustain themselves on their market-generated revenues. CED is a form of social development that uses business as a tool to achieve its goals. In this context of government cutbacks, organizations like A-Way play a significant social role, going beyond anything that the state could provide as an effective social service. Its strength is in its democratic practices and its position as a centre for personal and collective learning and power for a group that has traditionally been without voice. A-Way provides an example of an autonomous organization formed as a CED project to obtain social ends. There are many similar CED projects that have independent structures and use the market and business development but do not act like private sector businesses, particularly because of the priority given to internal democratic processes and social ends.

## QUESTIONS AND LIMITS OF CED

There are examples of CED organizations that have participated in organizing a strong voice at the local level through which those without economic power can participate in shaping local economic development or creating democratic workplaces. However, the mainstream of CED and social economy businesses is orientated towards much more traditional forms of business development, determined by marketplace demands and generating enough revenue to break even or make a profit. As well, as economic power has been concentrated supra-nationally, the local has very little power in controlling its economic direction, as investment is determined by those with little regard for the consequences of their choices on local life. CED thus sits in the same dilemma as most organizing practices; it can create innovative alternatives and possibilities, and it can open democratic spaces, but it has difficulty moving beyond the limits of government policy and market demands. CED has some potential as a vehicle for social change and a means of building a voice for those excluded from economic debates in our society. This is reflected in the definitions and in some of the practices that link economic initiatives with other social objects, like A-Way or some of the urban Aboriginal projects in Winnipeg (see Loxley et al., 2007). But more often I see CED, through the social economy, as a means of directing the community sector into an entrepreneurial mode without any vision of what can be gained by that process and without asking how business development can be a tool for social change.

In addition, CED is seen to a large extent as a strategy to reduce poverty, and as a form of economic development that can provide low-income people with a way to participate in the capitalist economy. However, it is ironic that one of the reasons for the increase in poverty is the withdrawal of state intervention in regulating the market. Meanwhile, the state and others (e.g., foundations) have called upon poor communities to use the same, less regulated market as a means of ameliorating local economic and social conditions. In other words, the state has lessened its responsibilities for dealing with the social consequences of capitalism and the related social inequalities, while the poor themselves are called upon to step up and become entrepreneurs within the capitalist system that has failed to meet even their most basic employment needs—a decent job with an adequate income. Can CED and associated small businesses do anything to ameliorate poverty without other extensive policies designed to redistribute income and wealth, and can they intervene to support in a large way alternative economic development and intervention in the private sector to limit exploitation? The danger of CED is that it is understood as a way for poor people to participate in and use the market economy rather than a way of organizing on the local level for power to influence state policy and at the same time create democratic options. Can CED practice generate adequate economic development at the local level to be an alternative that can ameliorate the consequences of economic restructuring? In an economic climate in which many new jobs tend to be low-wage or in the service sector, does CED act to reproduce the same type of low-wage work that is being created elsewhere?

These questions are played out as tensions facing CED practitioners. CED-related businesses and projects tend to pay very low wages or, as in the case of both A-Way and Resto-Pop, they benefit from the labour of those receiving social assistance. There are limited choices and often the work in these businesses is far more desirable for the employees than no work at all; yet, the issue of working conditions needs to be raised as a basic tension for CED businesses. In addition, as government has reduced spending on social programs, do CED practices that provide services act as a cheap replacement for government programs? For example, in recent years in Quebec there has been an increased demand for home-care services for a variety of groups. Traditionally, these services have been provided by government clinics in which the workers providing these services are unionized and have relatively permanent jobs as well as benefits. With the shift to the community sector, CED projects—in Quebec these have been referred to as the "social economy" (see Shragge and Fontan, 2000)—have included the provision of home-care services. As a consequence, these services have acted to replace those of the state and with far worse working conditions. This provides an example of how CED-type projects have been supported by government funding and as a consequence have created services that are far cheaper to operate with little long-term commitment. It is important to understand how CED practices can be used by the state for its own purposes. Perhaps not all CED activities play this role but this analysis reminds us of the contradictions of practice and how it can be used to achieve different ends.

CED projects have to confront the power of the market in determining their success and sustainability. Without a strong commitment to democratic processes, mobilization, and popular education, CED can result in the "commodification" of social development. In other words, it represents a shift from what were once considered non-market processes—public services including local development and the production of goods and services to be bought and sold. The early vision of the welfare state was to take essential goods, such as health care and education, out of the market and treat them as basic social rights. With the shift to the community sector and some of the CED strategies, there is a tendency to create business out of what used to be considered a public service. There is real pressure from the government's neo-liberal policy agenda to push CED practice in this direction. However, many of the diverse organizations that make up those involved in CED bring a rich tradition of opposition to this new context and they have not been entirely swallowed up. Yet the mainstream of CED is orientated towards much more traditional forms of business development that are determined by marketplace demands for profitability. As well, as economic power has been concentrated supra-nationally, the local has very little power in controlling its economic direction.

To conclude this section, I raise the following question: can CED, or social economy businesses, and the contemporary direction of community development transcend these limits, which are often imposed by financing structures that put organizations into specialized silos? Can they bridge social and economic development and service provision, as well as organize to demand social and economic justice at the same time? One organization illustrates the possibility: the Restaurant Opportunities Center. This organization has branches in eight cities in the USA, including Chicago, New York, and Miami. The following example comes from New York City. They explain their action goals as follows:

> worker organizing and empowerment, litigation, and public pressure, ROC-NY wins back unpaid wages and discrimination claims for these workers as well as important changes in the industry, such as vacations, paid sick days, mandated breaks, and more.... our victories also lay the ground in fostering leadership through our membership. Members are trained in campaign organizing and in harnessing the power and energy in their own co-workers to make the New York City restaurant industry a better place to work in. (Restaurant Opportunity Center, www.rocny.org, accessed July 26, 2012)

Leadership development is a key part of building an action organization. ROC has completed research on gender discrimination and, coupled with the growing number of female workers seeking to start campaigns against their employers for gender discrimination, has organized to develop long-lasting power for female restaurant workers. The ROC-NY Women's Committee is working to build the leadership of their fellow female restaurant workers and raise awareness around the gender discrimination plaguing this industry, thus providing an outlet for the voices of those who are neglected as well as making these voices heard to the public. If these were the only goals and practices then ROC would be similar to the many worker centres that exist today. However, they

combine this with many other practices, such as joining together policy analysis and worker education. For example, ROC-NY's Health and
Safety Committee works to educate restaurant workers about how to
avoid accidents, injuries, and pain while working in this dangerous industry. The committee also educates workers on their rights when accidents
do occur. As well, it is working to complete a major study of restaurant
workers' health and safety on the job, and it will be fighting to win paid
sick days and health insurance for restaurant workers. The organization's
Policy Committee creates worker-led policy initiatives to improve conditions for restaurant workers on city, state, and federal levels. Its training
programs through the Colors Hospitality Opportunities for Workers
(CHOW) Institute provide its members with the opportunity to obtain
living-wage jobs through free job training classes in both front- and back-
of-the-house restaurant skills. In addition, ROC has established a restaurant, Colors, that is run by former restaurant workers who survived the
attack on the World Trade Center. The restaurant is owned and managed
by the workers themselves. This example demonstrates that community
development and organizing can coexist within an organization. Both
methods can be used in a mutually strengthening manner to contribute
to a common goal of building power for a group of workers who are
usually powerless and creating democratic alternatives in the economy
and a strong voice for these workers.

## THE COMMUNITY DEVELOPMENT TRADITION: WORKING WITH THE CONTRADICTIONS

I have reviewed several ways in which the community development
approaches and practices are played out. The underlying belief of this
approach is in social consensus, which obscures basic questions of interest
and power. Its prominence is not really surprising given how the wider
social and economic context has shaped current social problems and the
possibilities of state response. Through the past years of globalization
and economic restructuring, the poor and the working class have been
hit hard. The prospects of change seem minimal and the options faced
by the community sector limited. Government programs have been cut
and in many instances pushed into the voluntary sector to be absorbed on
the cheap by overly busy community organizations. Except for periods of

mobilization—such as the student movement and its rallies in Quebec as well as, more globally, the Occupy movement—the opposition movements have been weakened and ignored by the arrogance of those promoting the corporate agenda. Trade unions, one traditional source of opposition, have seen their membership decline with the shift of traditional jobs away from Canada and the USA as well as the growth of irregular work. Survival is the mode for many unions and community organizations. The latter are faced with growing demands for services to meet more complex and difficult social problems, and they must do this with unstable funding. Community development practices provide a way out. They legitimate the role of community organizations, but government and, at times, corporately backed foundations make sure that their social change objectives remain subservient to these services. Governments have used their new collaborative relations with community organizations as a way to organize social provision and economic development, and to create the conditions to maintain harmony in a time of social deterioration. This is the bad news. I have deliberately overstated it in order to emphasize the direction of the pressures on community organizations to adapt to the new realities.

However, there are also opportunities. Community organizations, despite the models and practices they have adopted or been pressured to adopt, carry a legacy of opposition and contestation. This has originated from the many community-based organizations and services that mobilized their clients, staff, members, and boards to participate. Social action and the struggle for social justice coexist with the development model in a complex tension. The radical, explicitly oppositional traditions and ongoing practices continue to push, while the government and other sources of funding pull in a direction that neutralizes and professionalizes community organizations and uses them as cheap, flexible forms of social provision.

Despite the critique that I have raised, I do not to write off the practice of community development. These organizations and processes bring people together who share common issues and problems. They can become a context for practices that may not be the primary function of the organization but can contribute to social change. Describing the context in which political space can be built, Barker (1999) uses the concept of "activity centre" that consists of a person or a set of people at a place and time engaged in a program of activity along with the objects and environmental features to which the activity is coordinated.... they are units in which individual and collective intention and creativity abound. (p. 30)

Each activity setting is a process of activity that exerts forces on people within the setting. Activity settings are structured contexts of forces most immediately surrounding persons and their activities. (p. 51)

Thus, activity centres create a place of local politics where a variety of outcomes are possible. The benefit that can be derived from this perspective is that it bridges the individual and his/her action with the wider social and economic forces that shape their lives. These places provide linkages between these activities and the way that they function as a response to the wider social and political forces. This approach describes the interrelationship between the outside world and these settings. It acknowledges their potential to have an impact on processes of social change. Formal and informal processes in the organization provide the key in revealing their politics. If it were only the specific tasks carried out in community organizations that defined them, their contribution to social change would be minimal. However, the social processes in the organizations are the practices that move in other directions.

There are four traditions within the wider community movement that can act to promote a social change agenda within community development organizations—democracy, education, alliance-building, and mobilization. The community sector can draw upon them and they can be resurrected at the same time as organizations carry out other activities linked to services and economic development. Our connection to these traditions helps us to sustain a vision of why we organize. This vision is shaped by values of social justice and equality. One of the key roles of community organizing is to be part of a wider struggle for the redistribution of wealth and power. Organizations can provide the means for citizens to gain a voice.

Democracy is the key element. Community development, in all of its incarnations, has as a core belief its potential to involve its stakeholders in a democratic process. The rhetoric implies more than the practice, but the opportunity is there to be taken by leaders and staff of community organizations. They can insist on the active participation of residents, users of services, and staff in the decision-making processes in their organizations and the wider community. Creating a "democratic space" in which those without power can have a voice is a starting point in creating social change. In Browne's (2001) discussion of the social economy and other practices similar to it, he argues,

> Although they can be recuperated by neo-liberalism, such experiences present many immediate social benefits in the form of services and social inclusion. They are also one of many potential vehicles for the development of democratic capacities, of the ability to participate fully in society and to be self-governing—a process of cognitive and ethical transformation. They offer glimpses of a more democratic way of governance. (p. 98)

Without this dimension, community organizations become professional services, and those faced with difficult personal and social situations become passive clients. If democracy is the starting point, it cannot be the only goal. It provides the means of creating a culture of opposition based on active citizens. Up to this point, the argument has been similar to that of the writers cited earlier in the community development literature. The difference is that the processes that support democracy have to be extended outward towards external issues and structures. In other words, local democracy is the starting point for recapturing the other three traditions of community organizing.

Education, which happens in a variety of ways in community organizations, contributes to social change processes. It is important to understand these settings as sites of both potential and actual learning. Community organizers can gain understandings of these processes from the work of adult educators. Regardless of the formal mandates and goals of the settings, they provide opportunities in which participants at all levels can gain knowledge and use their experiences to contest their social situations and engage in a variety of new activities. Through these activities, it is possible to build social solidarity and to act in a collective way in promoting social change. Foley (1999) describes the type of learning in social movements as

> informal and often incidental—it is tacit, embedded in action and is often not recognized as learning. The learning is therefore often potential, or only half realised.... we need to expose it. In doing this it helps if we understand that people's everyday experience reproduces ways of thinking and acting which support the often oppressive status quo, but the same experience also produces recognitions which enable people to critique and challenge the existing order. (p. 4)

He argues that "the learning of oppositional, liberatory [ideologies] are central to the processes of adult education" (p. 4). Building on the everyday experiences of those participating in community organizations, a variety of educational opportunities are possible.

Cervero and Wilson (2001) discuss three views of political adult education that can be translated into the struggle for knowledge and power. The first they describe as "the political is personal"—a learner-centred view. It focuses on individual change through a consensus-based strategy. This parallels a service approach and, although drawing on the voices of those involved, it is limited to that. The second they define as "the political is practical"; this is similar to a pragmatic practice of community organizing. The goal here is to help people learn how to get things done and mobilize resources, but within the existing limits of power. In the context of community organizations, the lessons learned are about making limited changes and working for the interests of the organization or program. These lessons are also useful in preparing people to engage in the world of day-to-day politics, and at the same time they can promote a belief that politics is defined within those pre-existing limits. In contrast, the authors define the third viewpoint as "the political as structural," which believes in using adult education as a way to support the redistribution of power. This is the key dimension. In all aspects of work in the community, opportunities arise that lend themselves to provoking political discussion and unmasking power relations. Even if the primary function of the organization is not that of mobilization, people come for a variety of reasons related to wider social and political processes. Activities such as talks, workshops, and guest speakers on current issues provide an example of these activities. Foley (1999) notes that the learning opportunities are contradictory, providing both limits and possibilities of learning. In community development practice, there is a lot of pressure for social integration as opposed to social change, but the possibilities are there.

Educational practice can take many forms; it begins with an understanding that the problems and issues confronted locally have their origins in the wider society. They reflect patterns of inequality and injustice. The solutions cannot be found locally, and wider changes are necessary. Community organizations can play a role in promoting them. There are many creative ways to reach people that counter the conservative bias in the mainstream media, which attempts to convince us that there are no choices. Even if the primary mandate of an organization is service provision or development, it does not mean that there is no space to participate in other activities. The most effective way to do this is through participation in alliances with other organizations at the local level. By breaking down the isolation, organizations can step outside of their usual boundaries and take on new issues and activities. Alliances contribute to the creation of a base of social power and have the potential of going beyond the specific interests and problems of each organization and raising common concerns. An example of this process is a coalition of organizations in a working-class neighbourhood in Montreal that has drafted an alternative urban development plan to put forward local priorities and challenge those of the city administration.

Alliance building is key. Through it, organizations can join together to promote both local and global causes. At the local level these groupings can speak for the neighbourhood or sector and become legitimate local voices because they are the most representative bodies. The organizations—both service and voluntary—can move beyond their specific agendas and involve themselves in a process of building power, even if that is not their formal mandate. However, there is a danger in the process. These alliances become organizations of organizations regardless of whether they have a base of active members or are able to mobilize their constituency. Alliances, therefore, can become the representatives of communities rather than the catalyst for mobilization of residents. Organizations, through their staff or a few volunteers, substitute themselves for active citizens. This indirectly weakens the process. If the primary goal of the process is to build power through numbers of people, then representation by organizations undermines this goal. Further, organizations have a vested interest in survival, which can compromise the more explicit political agendas of others in the wider community.

If there is one underlying lesson on the potential of community organizing, it is the principle that large numbers of people working together with specific demands can have a voice in the process of social change. Howard Zinn, cited in a Z *Magazine* editorial, writes:

> When Sacco and Vanzetti faced death, and their lawyers came to them with hopeful new legal strategies, Vanzetti would answer: it won't help—they are determined to kill us—the only thing that will work is if a million people take to the streets and frighten the hell out of the system. That did not happen, and they were executed. (A simple plan, 2000, p. 7)

There is an important lesson here. It is the power of people that matters. There are many different paths to get there. Whether it is the recent struggle against tuition fees in Quebec, or the Occupy movement, or the numerous forms of opposition such as marches, sit-ins, and other methods of social disruption that were used to gain civil rights or better social or economic gains, it comes down to the power of numbers. That is the long and short of it. Trade unions can withhold their labour to try to negotiate better conditions. Community organizations have one real source of power and leverage—large numbers of people acting together. This might sound overly simplistic, but I believe that this is fundamental and has to be stated clearly so that when one gets to the complexities, the principle still stands out. This does not come easily, and it remains the challenge. It involves the other traditions—democracy, education, and alliance-building, and each of these contributes to the process. Other forms of practice and action create a critical consciousness and confidence in people. Any type of community organizing can have this potential. Thus, neither action organizing nor community development is inherently the best approach. It is the way they link to other movements and struggles that matters, and their contributions to democratic opportunities and a critical social analysis that make a difference in the longer term.

# CHAPTER SIX

# CONCLUSION: FIGHTING THE GOOD FIGHT— THE IMMIGRANT WORKERS CENTRE

In this concluding chapter, I will return to the question of what role community organizing and development plays in the process of social change. I will examine this question in two ways. The first is a presentation of the work of the Immigrant Workers Centre (IWC) in Montreal. I was co-founder of the centre in 2001. Since then my role has changed but I have been and continue to be active in most aspects of the centre's work. When I retired from Concordia University in 2012, I became a volunteer/ staff member there, and, as I write this, I am in the beginning stages of this role. I am privileged to receive a decent pension from the university that allows me to participate in an organization that carries left politics into the community. Part one of the conclusion will examine the centre as an example of on-the-ground work and the problems associated with it. Part two will be a final reflection on community and social change.

## THE IMMIGRANT WORKERS CENTRE

The IWC was founded as a response to two major issues that are at the core of all Western societies: global migration and the transformation of labour processes. These, in turn, reflect the transitions related to neo-liberalism, described in previous chapters. More broadly we need a historical perspective on Canada and immigration. It is important to remember that Canada was created by the two colonizing nations—France and England, with England displacing France. To create the modern nation state, two challenges had to be overcome. The first was the displacement and colonization of First Peoples, and the second was finding the labour power to create the infrastructure with which capitalists could create their fortunes in the "new world." The first was accomplished through disease, war, the church, and the system of reserves, and so on. The second was accomplished through the importation of labour, such as the Irish to build canals in Upper Canada and the Chinese to build the railways in the West. Migrant labour continues to be used either to carry out tasks that "residents" won't do or demand too much pay in order to do, or as a response to labour shortages. As we will see below, the tradition of abusing migrant labour continues today.

I will briefly summarize the general tendencies of immigration and work from the 1980s up to the current time period.[1] Immigration to Canada since the 1980s is part of the context that shapes the work of the IWC. From that period, immigration to Canada as to Europe has been mainly from countries of the "Global South," and largely non-White. The levels of education and training tend to be high; however, this education and training do not produce economic benefits. Immigrants to Canada end up in the worst and most precarious jobs, face unemployment and poverty levels much higher than native-born Canadians, and find that their credentials are not recognized and, if there is a chance they can be recognized, the process is long and difficult. As a consequence, many immigrants face very limited upward economic mobility. In addition, immigration policies set by the government have moved towards temporary labour programs. The main programs are the Live-in Caregiver Program (LCP), which brings in domestics mainly from the Philippines; the Seasonal Agricultural Workers (SAWP) Program, which brings in workers mainly from Latin America; and the generic Temporary Foreign Workers Program (TFWP), which brings workers from all over to do just about anything. In the TFWP, there are two categories of skills: high and

---

1 There are many sources to support this summary. For an introduction, see Choudry et al., *Fight Back: Workplace Justice for Immigrants* (2009).

low. As an immigrant in the high-skill category of the TFWP or within the LCP, it is possible to become a permanent resident under specified circumstances. There has been a significant expansion of the TFWP in recent years because the government considers temporary residents a means of fulfilling demands for difficult and low-wage work.

The current wave of immigrants arrived in the context of neo-liberal restructuring, which had two important implications. The first was the decline of blue-collar unionized labour with the corresponding growth of the service economy and the related increases of low-wage and precarious work. The second was the restructuring of the state that included budget cuts to many sectors and resulted in a greater demand for private services, particularly caregiving for children, the elderly, and those with disabilities. For many generations, government employment has meant stable, well-paid, and protected work. With cutbacks, these jobs have become very scarce. For the purposes of this discussion, then, the major consequence of neo-liberal restructuring has been a reduction in state regulation of employment and a reduction in the conditions of work both of which have generated a greater demand for low-wage workers. Another dimension has been reduced settlement services, including language-training courses and processes that support professional accreditation, which have forced many educated immigrant workers to seek employment at the bottom of the labour market. The responsibility of sending finances to their families back in their home countries is another reason immigrants have had to find work in whatever jobs are available. Thus, the combination of available jobs and expectations to "integrate" and support family members at home put enormous pressures on new arrivals to take any job they can land. These patterns which are present today and which vary across North America have led worker centres to create new forms of resistance and organizing.

## WORKER CENTRES

The IWC is an example of a broader movement of community-based labour organizing across North America. In the United States alone there are more than 130 centres. Fine (2006) states that these worker centres are community-based mediating institutions that provide support to communities of low-wage workers and that help them organize. The centres work primarily for newly arrived immigrants and have a broad agenda, with elements of service provision and policy-advocacy organizing. They are place-based rather than work-based, have strong ethnic and racial identification, and emphasize leadership development, internal democracy, and popular education. Organizers and leaders think globally and broadly and build coalitions. Organizationally, they mix formal structures with wider movement activities. They tend to be small with limited formal membership structures, but with an emphasis on identifying and supporting grassroots leadership (pp. 11–25). Gordon describes them as seeking "to build the collective power of their largely immigrant members and to raise wages and improve working conditions in the bottom-of-the-ladder jobs where they labor" (2005, p. 280).

These centres have emerged because labour unions have been unable to adequately address the conditions created by neo-liberal globalization. Fine (2006) describes these origins as linked to the following:

> difficult conditions under which low-wage immigrant workers toil are a result of a "perfect storm" of labor laws that have ceased to protect workers, little effective labor market regulation, and a national immigration policy that has created a permanent underclass of workers ... (p. 244)

The centres that Fine describes provide a range of activities that include building a movement through low-wage workers leadership development, popular education, and acting in solidarity with broader international movements; publicizing the issues low-wage workers face to a larger public in order to build sympathy and allies; seeking the enforcement of basic labour and unemployment laws and policies; working against racial and ethnic discrimination; and challenging issues related to immigrants' access to services. In general, these centres promote solutions for the situations that workers face through collective action that can alter the relations of power and win concrete victories. These centres draw on the traditions of labour and community organizing in order to build workers' power. One of the ways that they differ from unions is that their organizing targets include both private employers and governments. In both cases, the centres use campaigns and pressure tactics to win gains.

Their demands to governments are for greater regulation of the largely unregulated or difficult-to-regulate jobs at the bottom of the labour market. Another characteristic of the centres is the relationship they build with employment sectors such as the garment workers in Los Angeles or along the lines of shared ethnicity such as the Chinese workers in New York City. Some of the centres are affiliated with wider movements such as the Right to the City Alliance, presented in chapter 4, which links the local worker centre to movements demanding radical social change.

## A BRIEF HISTORY OF THE IWC

Montreal's IWC was founded in 2000 by a small group composed of Filipino-Canadian union and former union organizers and their allies of activists and academics. The idea of the IWC grew out of the experience of two of the founders who had worked as union organizers. They observed that much of their recruitment and education to support a union drive had to take place outside of the workplace and there were few locations where this process could happen, particularly in a collective way. Thus, the idea of the IWC was to provide a safe space outside of the workplace where immigrant workers could discuss their situation. Further, they had a critique of the unions themselves, arguing that once they got a majority to "sign cards" and join the union, the processes of education and solidarity built into the organizing process were lost as union "bureaucrats" came in to manage the collective agreement. Two elements attracted me to the IWC. The first was the possibility of linking radical political ideas and practice at the community level. I remember at the beginning how refreshing it was to talk to people who shared a left and Marxist critique of capitalism and the resulting inequalities of class, race, and gender, and who wanted to take these ideas and find a way to bring them into action at the local level. Second, at the time I had not read the literature on worker centres and the possibility of linking labour and community organizing was a challenging possibility. Traditional community organizing was separate from the organizing of labour through unions. At the beginning we did not have a specific action plan but a general framework and the idea that immigrant workers could be organized through an organization within their neighbourhood. In its first year, the IWC was able to secure a grant from the social justice fund of the Canadian Automobile Workers. The IWC then got to work providing ongoing education and critical analysis that went beyond the specific role of unions, as well as finding ways to address worker issues outside of the traditional union structures. Twelve years later, we are still here with the same general direction and politics.

The activities of the IWC cover labour rights counselling, popular education, and political campaigns that reflect the general issues facing immigrant workers. Labour education is a priority, providing workshops to organizations in the community and directly to workers in order to increase their skills and analysis. Workshops on themes such as the history of the labour movement, the Labour Standards Act, and collective organizing processes have been presented. Other educational activities include the "Skills for Change" program that teaches basic computer literacy while incorporating workplace analysis and information on rights. The goal is to integrate specific computer skills while supporting individuals in becoming more active in defending labour rights in their workplaces. French-language courses have recently been added, and IWC's office provides direct service to individuals. The issues brought into the office include unfair dismissal, unpaid wages, and unpaid overtime. Staff and volunteers accompany these workers as they take these grievances to the Commission des normes du travail (labour standards board) or other government agencies that are supposed to regulate general labour conditions. Over the years, many workers have won their claims. In addition, when a worker comes in, we ask her/him if there are others in the same situation and facilitate collective action, often building a group to file a grievance. More broadly, an ongoing link between the struggles of immigrant workers with other social and economic struggles as a way to build alliances is a priority. In addition, the IWC supports union organizing in workplaces where there is a high concentration of immigrant workers. The IWC, as an organization, crosses traditional boundaries and has characteristics of a social movement through its participation in the wider movements for migrant workers' justice. As well, having a board of directors and providing services and educational programs to workers is more in the tradition of non-profits. The IWC has a clear vision of itself as a social-change organization engaged in collective action that emerges from the experiences lived by immigrant workers themselves.

Campaigns are viewed not only as a way to make specific gains for immigrant workers but also as a way to educate the wider community about the issues they face. For example, the first campaign, in 2000, was to defend a domestic worker, here under the Live-in Caregiver Program, against deportation. The IWC played a support role to PINAY, an organization of domestic workers from the Philippines. This domestic worker had been unable to complete her twenty-four months of live-in work because her employer fired her when she became pregnant, and she was unable to find a new employer willing to have her live-in with her infant son. In addition to winning the campaign, the issue of importing labour as "indentured servants" was brought into the public sphere and many community organizations and unions became involved in this issue. Another example is when, along with many other groups in Quebec, the IWC became involved in a campaign to reform the Labor Standards Act in 2002. Because many immigrant workers do not work in unionized shops, the Labor Standards Act provides one of the few actions that non-unionized workers' can take against their employers. The IWC brought to the campaign specific concerns, including the exclusion of domestic workers from the act and the difficulty they have in accessing information about their rights. In 2003 ICW won a victory for the implementation of policy changes that would include the coverage of domestic workers in the reformed Labor Standards Act. However, despite the reforms won in this province-wide campaign, the act still has many inadequacies in protecting workers in precarious and irregular jobs. The ICW continues to campaign for the extension of health and safety legislation in the act to cover domestic workers.

Another aspect of the IWC's work has been its contribution to the organizing of cultural events with political content. The first was an International Women's Day event organized in 2001. A coalition of immigrant women of diverse origins organized a cultural event, panels, and a march to emphasize the concerns of immigrant women and to foster international solidarity. This event is now held annually and through its success has increased the profile and the issues faced by immigrant women within the wider women's movement in Quebec. The first Mayworks events, a community/union festival celebrating labour struggles through the arts, were launched for May Day of 2005. The festival was initiated by the IWC and found collaboration from within trade unions and the wider activist community. The festival has been held annually since then and includes a community event in a local park as its core. The Mayworks event of 2011 celebrated the tenth anniversary of the IWC and more than 200 people participated.

The following is a more detailed example of how the IWC develops its intervention. With globalization and the shifting of jobs to developing countries, the textile sector in Montreal has been in serious decline. Once a prosperous and key sector of employment for immigrants back in the early twentieth century, the sector has recently lost many of its jobs to "off-shore" production in poorer countries. Since its beginning, the IWC has dealt with cases of workers in this sector. Often, these cases have concerned unjust dismissal and lack of representation either because there were no unions or the unions were weak and did not adequately represent their members. Since 2007, there has been an increase in the number of workers reporting job loss to the IWC. One company in particular came to the attention of organizers: Lamour Hosiery Manufacturing. There had already been cases brought through the IWC against Lamour for its working conditions, such as the front door being kept locked and chained during the night shift. Under these conditions, workers were always in danger of being trapped in the case of an industrial fire because escape routes were limited. Often those doing piecework were not paid when machines broke down and they could not produce quotas. Workers were forced to have meals at their stations while they continued to work, which meant that they virtually had no breaks. All of this was made worse by a union set up in 2004 and believed by many workers to be a "pro-management" union, preventing workers from organizing themselves and pressuring for changes in working conditions. This time, however, it became clear that the company was shutting down production in Montreal and offering no compensation to the workers. A group of twenty-five workers, who had on average been working for this company for more than ten years and some for more than twenty, began meeting. Another fifty members joined the group at the beginning of August 2008. The question was, How would they respond to layoffs?

The IWC met the committee of workers from Lamour, at which time it became clear that returning to their old jobs was impossible and there were workers from other factories in the sector who reported similar layoffs. As well, Lamour had become a very profitable company for its owners, boasting that it was a leader in the apparel industry and had operations in China, Pakistan, Bangladesh, and India with over 2,500 workers worldwide. A long-time partner of the retail giant Walmart, it had recently broken into the US manufacturing market in July 2007 by taking over Terramar Sports, a company based in Tarrytown, New York.

Through these discussions, the workers decided on one significant demand: fair compensation for the years of loyalty they had shown the company. The situation was complex. If the company had shut down entirely or laid off large numbers of workers, all at the same time, the workers would have been eligible for "collective layoff benefits." The company chose, however, to lay off workers in small numbers systematically, avoiding collective layoffs and the related benefits. The workers chose as a strategy to pressure both the Labour Relations Tribunal for inadequate labour representation and the Labour Standards Board. They called for these bodies to intervene and treat layoffs as collective so that the workers would be eligible for much higher benefits. At the same time, a wider committee of workers from Lamour and a couple of other factories facing similar conditions joined forces and began to develop a policy that would cover all workers in the declining textile sector. This campaign involved workers who were not unionized or were represented by weak or pro-boss unions. In contrast to the situation at Lamour, another company that had closed in Montreal with a strong union saw the workers receive a decent compensation package. In the end, many workers from Lamour received increased benefits because of the pressure exerted on the government. These were limited, however, because the benefits were tied to a family income test, which meant that if a spouse was working the benefits were reduced.

The situation of workers at Lamour is typical of what other workers coming to the IWC have to face. They, too, have experienced and continue to experience the failure of government institutions that regulate the labour market. State policies governing the labour market were established during the 1950s, a period in which most jobs were stable and regular. Today, jobs in the textile industry are increasingly irregular (uncertain shifts, reduced shifts, and so on) as management is driven to reduce labour costs. The shift in this sector makes it difficult to regulate the workplace through existing policies and programs. Without the collective action of the Lamour workers, there would have been no recourse for the workers and they would have received little compensation with their layoff notices. News of this campaign travelled through word of mouth and ethnic media so that workers from other factories and even other cities began contacting the IWC with similar situations. Although it is difficult, the way forward is through political campaigns that not only challenge employers but also government bodies that are supposed to protect workers' rights.

## CURRENT PRIORITIES AND CURRENT CAMPAIGNS

I will present one current area of IWC's priorities to illustrate how the organization works on the issue of casual labour. The IWC has two priority groups that reflect changes in how employers and the state are reorganizing the labour market and increasing the precarious nature of employment, while at the same time indirectly attacking working-class power. Two groups of immigrant workers are particularly vulnerable— those working through temporary employment agencies and those coming to Canada through various temporary employment programs. The following discussion will focus on those working through temporary employment agencies.

Temporary employment agencies cover a spectrum of situations, including high-skill, high-paying professional jobs. Our focus here is on those agencies supplying the low-paid, precarious sectors of the economy. However, these agencies are no longer on the periphery of the labour market. According to Statistics Canada (No 63–252Xo, 2008), between 1993 and 2008, the number of registered agencies grew from 1,191 to 5,077, an increase of 325 per cent and, since 2001, the revenue from this exploitation increased by 80 per cent to $9.2 billion (cited in a press release of Au bas de l'échelle and the Immigrant Workers Centre). This does not include many agencies that are not registered. A research document developed by Au bas de l'échelle describes some of the ways that agencies undermine labour standards and conditions of work that contribute to the growth of precarious labour. They include substandard working conditions; the unequal treatment of workers in the same workplace, some employed directly by the employer and others through temp agencies; systematic infractions of the labour code by some agencies;

abusive clauses in the contract the agency requires workers to sign; the lack of responsibility of employers; and low safety standards that result in high levels of accidents among temp workers. Employers have also established their own agencies, which hire specifically for them. One strategy agencies use is to have more than one registered company and move workers from one to the other to avoid payment of overtime.

All of these are problematic, but one important consequence of contract work is that the employer is not responsible for the working conditions in his/her place of work, which has huge implications on the recourse for workers. In theory, workers regardless of whether or not they work for a temp agency have recourse through labour standards if there is a violation of their rights. However, according to the labour standards board, it is not clear who is responsible and each situation is determined according to many different variables. Thus, this uncertain and legally complex situation acts to deter complaints. As a consequence, employers are protected from complaints against them and they have no responsibility for workplace conditions. Because of this lack of recourse, temp agency workers are often exposed to high-risk jobs without proper equipment and training. Another dimension that is particularly troubling is that Emploi Québec, the government agency that manages social assistance and job referrals, has been referring immigrant workers to temp agencies, thus providing a pool of immigrant labour for these kinds of jobs.

The IWC sets its priorities based on the issues that workers bring into the centre. Over the last two years, many workers have been coming in asking for help related to problems they faced with temporary employment agencies. Their jobs were diverse, with many were working in health and social services, warehouses, agriculture, and so on. The following is an example:

The IWC helped a group of temporary agency workers file a complaint with the Commission des normes du travail (CNT). After working at a food processing plant for over a year, they were collectively dismissed, first by the employer where they worked, then by the agency that placed them giving them the reason that there was lack of work. Neither the company nor the temp agency provided prior notice and, according to Quebec labour standards, the workers were owed several weeks of pay in place of the notices. This was on top of unpaid regular wages for their last week of work as well as unpaid overtime. Their first hurdle was getting their claims accepted at the CNT and, once they were accepted, they had the complicated task of determining who exactly their employer was and who was responsible for the violation of the labour standards. When the labour board finally determined that the temp agency was responsible, it was too late as the agency had disappeared. The CNT could not enforce the labour standards on an agency that officially closed its doors overnight. According to the workers, the agency simply reopened under a new name. The food processing company got away without compensating the workers.

The challenge is how to organize temp agency workers. I will use this example to discuss some of the problems and realities of mobilization and building organization. This process is ongoing at the IWC and the outcome is uncertain. From the outset, the goal has been to organize an association of temp agency workers that will give them the power to challenge their employers-agencies and places of work, demand justice, and represent themselves in their struggle for economic justice. There have been several stages in this process. One part-time employee at the IWC was a former temp agency employee at the warehouse of a large dollar store chain, where he worked for a couple of years. The IWC decided to target this warehouse where up to 200 workers had jobs, all contracted through agencies and many of them recent immigrants from Africa. The conditions were difficult and the workers had little protection. The IWC distributed leaflets at the subway stations these workers used at the end of their shifts. The leaflets presented the position of the IWC and Au bas de l'échelle, emphasizing that the temp workers had rights. Our outreach team met some of the workers and we decided to call a meeting, inviting a lawyer from the CNT to discuss the rights of temp agency workers. About thirty workers showed up for the discussion. The lawyer raised the complication of deciding who the employer was and who was responsible for labour standard violations—was it the agency or the workplace employer? This ambiguity demonstrated how difficult it was to proceed with grievances either individually or collectively. Another problem quickly arose. Both the agency and the warehouse supervisors got wind that workers were beginning to organize and sent one of the leaders of the group to work somewhere else. This individual had spoken to many workers, mobilized them for the meeting, and spoke at the meeting. He had a graduate degree in occupational health and safety but could not find any other work except through a temp agency. The following meeting was not as successful because many workers had moved to other jobs or had returned to school part time.

As this was happening, there was an exposé of temp agency work and the poor working conditions on a major television network. Au bas de l'échelle (ABE) and the IWC called a press conference to discuss the realities of this work and to demand government intervention. Within IWC and ABE, discussions continued about launching a campaign for reform. There were several reasons for this. For the IWC, the goals of this campaign were as follows: to bring workers together from different sectors and communities; to have a real impact on people's lives and not be abstract; to be able to build more workplace fight-backs, while building leadership among immigrant workers themselves. For ABE, public pressure on the government could strengthen its lobbying, and for both organizations, public awareness was part of any kind of effort for change. The key element was to demand greater government regulation of temp agencies. The two key demands, which did not exclude other issues, were as follows: make it mandatory that agencies receive an operating permit and that both the agency and the employer be co-responsible for conditions in the workplace. The registration of these agencies would be one means of forcing them to be accountable for their actions and to end fly-by-night operations, such as the one described above. However, the more important demand was joint responsibility of the agency and the employer for the conditions of work. As it currently stands, when the labour standards board processes a grievance, it has to determine who is responsible and it treats each case uniquely. So besides the usual personal risk of job loss, and so on, that workers face when grieving against their bosses, the uncertainty of who is responsible further deters action.

For the campaign, several directions were initiated. The first was to get unions, community organizations, and women's organizations to endorse the demands. This was highly successfully and we received backing from more than 200 organizations. On May Day 2011, a pamphlet prepared by the IWC and ABE was distributed during the annual march informing workers and political allies about the issue and the campaign. As well, the IWC and ABE prepared a petition for workers to sign in support of these demands. For the IWC, this enabled a small core group of agency workers to talk to people and get signatures. It was part of a process of engaging these workers in the campaign. At this stage, at the IWC, there remained a small committed group of agency and former agency workers that had begun to play a leadership role. This included members of Dignidad Migrante, a group of Latin American workers, with many members working through temporary agencies in agriculture and greenhouses.

The next stage in the campaign was an action on the International Day for Decent Work in October. The goals were to continue public education through the media, present the demands publically to the minister of labour, and for the IWC to build the leadership of its emerging core group. A bus tour brought some agency workers, IWC and ABE staff and volunteers, journalists, and some allies to agencies and workplaces. Workers from the IWC spoke about their experiences and the issues of temp agencies. The bus tour ended at the minister's downtown office and a demonstration and banners greeted participants in the tour. The petitions and letters of support were taken to the minister's office by an aide because security would not let our delegation into the building. Since that action, the priority at the IWC has been to build a core group of leaders who are employed thorough temp agencies. The process has been slow. The workers and staff have drafted a proposal for an agency workers association and have begun regular meetings. Staff and volunteers at the IWC have continued to reach out. Gradually new workers are finding the centre and are bringing grievances against employers. The strength of the group is the cohesion of its leaders from different backgrounds and their commitment to building an organization of temp workers that will engage in the process of challenging employers, agencies, and government. One of the difficulties is finding a time for everyone to meet. This and other issues will be discussed below.

## CHALLENGES AND LESSONS

A core belief within IWC is that change can only happen if there is an organization of immigrant workers that can build power and represent themselves against both employers and state agencies and policies. It is a difficult process, and has had some successes and faced many challenges.

What are the difficulties, challenges, and barriers to organizing immigrant workers and particularly those in the most precarious jobs such as temp agency workers? Organizing workers requires connections between the people who are being organized; this is the glue that brings them together. These connections are usually linked to their workplaces, neighbourhoods, and identities, such as a shared culture. In working with immigrant workers in the context described above, not one of these three categories exists. Many of the worker centres in the United States are based on sector or country of origin. The groups organized at the IWC do not share these categories. Further, in the case of temp agency workers, there is little permanency in one place of employment. In some ways, if employers were to design a system that would make it almost impossible for workers to organize, the temp agency model would be one. In addition, as Crawford et al. (2006) point out:

> With the spread of precarious employment, more and more workers cycle in and out of work; equally central, with privatizations and the down-loading of a range of social services onto households and communities, more and more workers also juggle multiple demands on their time, moving between paid and unpaid work. (p. 356)

This was particularly evident in the case of the textile workers, who despite making gains in the conditions of their layoffs through collective action, disbanded as a group when each of them found new directions in their lives and pursued different interests—French-language courses, retirement, new jobs, and so on. Many of the temp agency workers who have participated in IWC activities have changed places of work, have moved homes, have attempted to requalify for other jobs by taking courses, or have changed their work hours. This contributes to instability and makes it difficult for many to continue their involvement.

Another barrier that discourages organizing is risk-taking in the workplace, including the huge stake new immigrant workers have in keeping their jobs. Jobs are perceived to be extra important in the pathway to permanent residency and in the long-term goal of attaining citizenship. Many workers out of necessity send remittances to family in their home countries. Losing a job means not only the loss of income for the individual but also for his/her family. At another level, the political climate after many years of neo-liberal triumph and a weak opposition movement have contributed to a sense of pessimism about what can be achieved through organizing, given the trade-off of risk and time, particularly for immigrant communities working in low-wage precarious work. What can be gained by contesting an unjust workplace situation versus the risk of losing the job altogether? Many only come to the IWC when they have been unjustly dismissed, rather than dealing with situations that might have led to the job loss, because the risk is just too high.

In the work at the IWC, these challenges are evident. However, despite these challenges there are workers who will contest their situations. One of the underlying issues is the demand for respect. It is not always the small material gain that motivates an individual to contest the situation but a sense of personal dignity. Given the challenges, how does the IWC approach organizing? The temp worker agency is a good example. Building a core group of leaders is the first step. Leaders are those individuals who have come to the IWC in a variety of ways, and who work in a particular target area, for example, temp agencies, and are willing and able to mobilize others. These leaders become the core of an organization of temp workers. This core group of workers has prepared a proposition about an organization of temp workers with a membership list. There is an emerging group of leaders from different backgrounds, countries of origin, and places of work and has both status and non-status members. The process is to gradually recruit a membership, using educational meetings and social events. IWC supports this process through the use of staff and volunteer time by providing help with individual and collective cases such as unfair dismissal or unpaid wages. One project that was initiated by the IWC and supported by a private foundation was the use of radio and podcasts to document the situations of temporary foreign and temp agency workers. These can be used as tools of public education and on radio stations listened to by these workers. Part of the process is to train workers to do the interviews with others, and thus build connections and skills in the group. The posting of interviews and listening to them on the radio is an effective way of reaching other workers. (These can be heard by visiting the IWC website, http://iwc-cti.ca.) There is a frustration at times because extensive outreach for meetings generates few new members, but there is also realism among the organizers and leaders in the group about the challenges presented above. What is the appropriate structural form to build an organization such as the IWC? One of the challenges facing worker centres as Fine (2006) mentions is building a membership organization. Organization-building that gives power to immigrant workers is a difficult undertaking. We have seen in both cases described above the problems with maintaining the participation of workers after the initial mobilization. People aiming to take on the status quo in an effort to promote justice need to consider some fundamental organizational issues: What structure would work best for our purposes in the current context? What kind of financial or other resources do we need and/or have access to? What are the structures of accountability?

Organizational structure has far-reaching implications. It can be a mirror of the kind of participatory, open organizational structure we want to see—or not. It can make the work more efficient, responsive, and effective—or not. It can create opportunities for diverse engagement within a common struggle—or not. Which way these things swing depends on the choices we make in structuring our organizations. At the grassroots level, organizing begins with people sharing common interests and coming together for mutual aid, information, and strategy-building. People may consciously decide to form a collective that is loosely structured but with agreed-upon principles for decision-making and ways of working. This form may continue permanently if the group decides that this is the way it wants to work. It has advantages. First, it reflects an appropriate structure for mobilization and education on a single issue or campaign. Also, because it is easy to maintain, it requires few resources and does not have to make compromises if it decides to find ways to raise money. We should not underestimate the importance of informal collective action.

Asef Bayat (2010), for example, discusses these processes in Third World cities under authoritarian regimes, using the concept of the "quiet encroachment of the ordinary" to describe how informal processes are used to appropriate urban space and challenge ruling relations. However, if organizations want to find support to pay rent, overhead, and organizers, they usually have to move in a more formal direction. As groups become more formalized, they tend to go one of two ways: the route of the NGO model with a board of directors and stockholders that are composed of supporters but not necessarily those directly involved in the issue at hand, or the route of a union model. The first model is similar to a corporate structure, if one substitutes "stockholders" with "members." There is a concentration of power with the board and staff, and limits to membership participation and involvement. The trade union model has a clear membership that makes decisions and sets direction. ACORN, which was discussed in chapter 4, provides an example of this model. Both can be democratic or restrictive. Unions and organizations using that type of structure can become highly professionalized and staff-directed while maintaining the formal membership structure. Beyond mobilizing people at a local level, many organizations identify a need to join forces at a higher level through federated structures, campaign-oriented coalitions, or temporary alliances. These alliances can be highly effective but they can also leave out the membership or base of the organizations.

Regardless of the structures that organizations use, formalization raises many issues, as it has important political implications. Many community organizers and social movement activists are concerned about the "NGOization" of movements and struggles—that is, their institutionalization, professionalization, depoliticization, and demobilization (Kamat, 2004; INCITE! Women of Color Against Violence, 2007; Veltmeyer, 2007). Sangeeta Kamat (2004) argues that this process is driven by the neo-liberal policy context in which NGOs operate. Organizations must demonstrate managerial and technical capabilities to administer, monitor, and account for project funding. Mass-based organizations of movements that represent their demands themselves through various forms of political mobilization have often been overshadowed or displaced by organizations that claim to represent the poor and marginalized, but in fact have no mass base or popular mandate. While there are exceptions, many NGOs and community organizations create and become enmeshed and invested in maintaining webs of power and bureaucracy, which divert energy and focus away from building oppositional movements for social change.

The IWC has a hybrid approach. There are several instances of this within it. There is a formal board of directors. It is there because the organization is incorporated as a non-profit organization. The board has two functions: to make sure the centre can remain open, and to support staff in their roles. The board is open and membership includes union staff members, academics, political allies, and workers. In addition, the weekly team meetings are made up of staff, students from disciplines such as social work who are carrying out field placements, and volunteers. In the meetings, tasks for the week are discussed as well as problems. Most important are the workers themselves. As the two earlier examples discussed, workers are mobilized around specific issues that bring them into contact with the centre. These contacts are usually a consequence of ongoing outreach targeted to specific groups of workers. As a result, workers contact the centre usually with grievances and staff and volunteers respond either by working individually or helping the worker to recruit others in the same situation to begin a process of collective action.

There are many benefits to the process. It creates a structure of support for the work and allows the setting of priorities to come from the experiences of workers who team up with the centre. The process of leadership development, the helping of workers to become spokespeople, and a commitment to collective decision-making on strategy and tactics keep the grassroots work democratic. The goal of the centre is to build a strong organized voice for immigrant workers, led by them and supported by the organizing team and the board. However, most of the work to date has been short-term, lasting only as long as the issue. Many of those who were involved stay in touch with the centre and come to events like the tenth anniversary celebration. The work with the temp agency workers is different. The IWC is in process of setting up an association that can act on cases, specific conflicts, build leadership and analysis, and work on longer-term campaigns. Its structure is loose and it has a group of leaders and a growing list of members. Outreach and mobilization are still the main activities and, along with building connections between the workers, remain the top priorities. It is a work in progress.

## CONCLUSIONS: CHALLENGES AND POSSIBILITIES

Organizing labour in the community is a new form that gives voice and some power to immigrant workers, who are the most marginalized group in the labour market. With some exceptions, labour has been the domain of the union movement. However, with the changes described above, worker centers have been founded to counter the difficulties faced by unions in the restructured labour market. There has often been a distinction drawn between direct service and organizing. Many community organizations are pushed to provide direct service by their funders and, as a result, their organizing activities become secondary. The IWC and similar community centres see individual service as a key way to attract people to their organizations. For an individual to step forward and challenge his/her boss on an issue of working conditions is an act of courage and is inherently political. And because individual problems are based in a workplace and in a policy context, they are often shared by others and form the basis for collective action. So, for organizations like the IWC, the issues brought in by community members contribute to building collective action and campaigns.

For community and labour organizing in general, working with individuals is the starting point to initiate collective action. It is often impossible to organize directly in the workplace because of the precarious nature of many of the jobs of immigrant workers. Therefore, the target of their campaigns has been the state, demanding improvements in conditions for everyone at the bottom end of the labour market. Policy-oriented campaigns that demand state intervention such as improvements in labour standards or extending coverage of health and safety are the result. In the current climate, in which immigrants are used as a cheap pool of labour that can be brought into workplaces or excluded as needed, new strategies that challenge exploitation are necessary. The emergence of worker centres with an immigrant membership along with strong unions is a start on the road to building a class movement for workplace justice alongside the union movement.

I have been immersed in the IWC for many years, and I have learned a great deal about organizing and about the situations faced by immigrant workers. I have also witnessed courageous individuals, at times without status, willing to take on both employers and state policies that are unjust. The IWC is an organization that has been able to fight for social and economic justice and challenge employers and the state. It has not compromised on its goals. The daily practices are shaped by the context of what workers face and the limited options available to them, such as the labour standards legislation. Within these we have had some victories, such as compensation for workers unjustly dismissed or back wages that were unpaid. These fights take a lot of energy and time and the victories for either individuals or groups of workers are small. The larger policy issues are harder and campaign victories have been very limited. These campaigns shift public understanding and push issues forward. In a period in which many community organizations and their coalitions mobilize to defend past gains and to fight against cutbacks, making new demands to go beyond what is runs against the grain of most organizations in the community sector. However, campaigns are educational and are the way to build leadership and a collective voice for immigrant workers. These are realities and, despite the frustrations, the IWC has stayed the course and is an organization of struggle and opposition, always willing to accompany workers in their fight for justice.

The IWC has been an intersecting point between generations of activists and organizers, social movements and local organizing. Many younger people who became politicized through the anti-globalization movement, or who have been involved in student politics or the Occupy movement have sought out the IWC for volunteer experiences. They see the IWC as a way to bring their movement experiences into longer-term local work. Their energy has been positive and the IWC provides a learning opportunity for how to take radical politics into working-class communities. In addition, the IWC is a crossover point between social movements and local work. The centre is used for a variety of meetings for immigrant groups, social movements, and solidarity organizations. This has contributed to an organizational culture in which the bridge between social movements and local work is crossed. For example, the IWC and students organized the pot-banging demonstrations in the IWC neighbourhood during the "Quebec Spring" in support of the student strike and in opposition to the repressive government legislation.

With the above perspectives, one of the key questions to ask is how has the IWC supported these activities? This has been one of the ongoing difficulties of the centre. As an advocacy/organizing centre, we are not eligible for a charity number and therefore cannot access many sources of funding—for example, Centraide (United Way). In addition, we have not been able to get recurrent money like other "social rights" organizations in Quebec. Part of the answer is that the older organizations were there earlier and this program has not been expanded. The IWC has used many different avenues, such as participating in specific research projects that have brought money to the centre as a research partner, and working with university professors on dissemination of research results, such as one project on temporary foreign workers and the related policies and programs. The IWC has received periodic government grants for events or specific projects. One of the ways we keep the centre going is through appeals to individuals and trade unions. Unions are an important ally, and many of the IWC's goals are shared within the union movement, which understands how programs like agency work and Temporary Foreign Workers are undermining their strength. Fundraising is ongoing and time-consuming. However, it is a way to talk to many people about the centre's work and we have found many supporters. Workers themselves are often generous. One day a woman came into the centre to thank the IWC for helping her husband win reinstatement in a job from which he was unjustly fired. His victory had important implications for his pension. She donated a substantial amount of money. Similarly, in the summer of 2012, we sent out an emergency appeal and many workers in the Temporary Foreign Workers program made generous donations. An autonomous and left-wing community organization will have trouble in the current climate. Part of the reason for our success is the commitment of our staff and volunteers, who are at the IWC out of political and social dedication, and continue to work at times without salary. The IWC continues to be an organization of struggle, but the lack of funding has been a cloud over the centre and an ongoing issue. At a personal level, one of the roles I play is to help with fundraising. I would rather use my time for other things, but autonomy and protecting our orientation requires that staff, volunteers, and board members participate in finding resources for the IWC.

## FINAL THOUGHTS

Studs Terkel, the great American journalist, was asked on a Public Radio broadcast on October 24, 2005, how he understood community. This is part of his answer.

> My own beliefs, my personal beliefs, came into being during the most traumatic moment in American history: the Great American Depression of the 1930s. I was 17 at the time, and I saw on the sidewalks pots and pans and bedsteads and mattresses. A family had just been evicted and there was an individual cry of despair, multiplied by millions. But that community had

a number of people on that very block who were electricians and plumbers and carpenters and they appeared that same evening, the evening of the eviction, and moved these household goods back into the flat where they had been. They turned on the gas; they fixed the plumbing. It was a community in action accomplishing something.... And this is my belief, too: that it's the community in action that accomplishes more than any individual does, no matter how strong he may be.

The community of the 30s and 40s and the Depression, fighting for rights of laborers and the rights of women and the rights of all people who are different from the majority, always paid their dues. But it was their presence as well as their prescience that made for whatever progress we have made. (Terkel, 2005)

In many ways this summarizes the argument that I have been making throughout the book. Through collective action within community, people build power to resist and to challenge the power of the state or private capital. As I discussed in chapter 1, it is about building opposition and counter-power to the dominant forces such as capital, patriarchy, and racism in their diverse expressions in everyday life. In contrast, I used the term integration to describe an approach used to increase people's participation in the system as it is or to enlarge resources or distribute some goods a little more fairly without challenging the basic assumptions of the system itself. Integration is those practices that support the maintenance of the fundamental power relations of our society and are designed to help people either meet their needs or make gains within the existing structures and processes. It assumes that the system can expand to accommodate and bring people into either the job or the lifestyle defined by corporate capitalism. It does not question the limits and the competitive nature of the system. Organizing within this approach does not go beyond either the limitation of local, winnable demands or service and development.

Opposition can also be expressed through the creation of "autonomous" spaces and projects. Breton et al. (2012) discuss the emergence of these organizations out of the protest movement linked to the movement to challenge the globalization of capital. They describe the organizations as feminist/pro-feminist, anti-authoritarian, and often explicitly anarchist. They tend to be organized through small affinity groups with organizational forms that are non-hierarchical. The activities are wide-ranging from cultural to social, such as self-managed farms, alternative bookstores, free schools, and show spaces. In addition, they engage in protests using creative tactics when mobilizing for these activities. These groups are often small but represent "the hope for fundamental social change [that] lies in their ability to show by example that self-governance and self-organization are not just desirable but also enjoyable and achievable in the present moment" (Breton et al., 2012, p. 159). Bluestockings, a workers cooperative bookstore in New York City, shares this orientation. It sees its project as testing the hypothesis that "autonomous space facilitates the production of new social relations in the struggle against capitalism" (Kanuga and Bluestockings Book Store, 2010, p. 20). One can argue that these projects end up as radicals speaking to radicals and do not reach out beyond those circles. However, the goals are wider and these spaces have become points of resistance and mobilization for protest. One advantage is that they continue between periods of protest and they share this continuity with community organizations, like Right to the City Alliance, the IWC, and FRAPRU, each of which has continuity and contributes to wider mobilizations.

Community organizations have the potential to carry progressive values into practice. Despite all of the pressures they face to collapse into some kind of politically innocuous service entity, many have managed to use the resources from the state and/or private foundations to contribute to ongoing political education and mobilization for ordinary people to struggle for social and economic justice. FRAPRU provides an example. It is not easy to balance the demands of those funding these organizations with the traditions of social change and wider activism. Democratic processes to mobilize people for action, education, and agitation are key elements within these and other community organizations. Further, it is important that organizers not only be aware of the core structures and processes of global capitalism but also that organizations name the problem and the necessity for a democratic and participatory system based on economic and social justice.

Community organizations can contribute to the building of a wider oppositional political culture. Community-based organizers need to understand their work as transcending the local. The political potential of community emerges when there is an emphasis on working "within a place," rather than "about a place." Communities are often limited by boundaries, usually geographic, or based on identity or specific interests. Their activities are thereby limited to local processes, and there is often little interest in going beyond these boundaries. This work should be the starting point, but not the ultimate goal. The community serves as a point of entry, but issues faced by all organizations go beyond the local. A broader movement is necessary to challenge the economic, social, and political power that keeps capitalism functioning and benefiting the minority. A movement of the majority is required for this to happen. Local work is a way to bring people together on a variety of concerns and with analysis of the connections between local and wider issues as well as real connections between local organizing and broader movements and alliances. At times these relations are expressed through protest movements, such as local groups mobilizing members for Occupy activities or the protests supporting the student strikes in Quebec this year. However, these movements are often short-lived and local organizing continues after these protest waves have run their course. At the same time, the local forms a base that can be mobilized for wider protests and contestation of power. Thus, the key is the connection between local work and broader struggles and the important role of the local in mobilizing, educating, and building leadership and winning local battles, and not isolating these gains and processes from the broader task of building opposition. Local work provides the political opportunity of engaging with people in a variety of situations—labour, housing, gender issues, etc.—and helping build connections between people who share a common situation, a common analysis of why, and common forms of action to do something about it. In a recent conversation I had with someone at the IWC, I told her that organizing is not complicated; it is about relationship-building with people who come to the centre, providing them with options for action, and then finding ways of sustaining it. There is often discussion about building critical consciousness, and this is important, but what we have found at the centre is that while people understand their class, racialized, and gendered positions, the more important goal is finding possibilities of action to challenge the day-to-day expressions of these relations and of building opposition to the capitalist system that creates them—that is, linking the everyday struggles to the wider struggles. This is the challenge. Although community organizations cannot do it by themselves, they provide a base for the wider movements and connections between the moments as they rise and fall. These connections are essential, as is the ongoing day-to-day work that builds the longer-term base for a sustained opposition.

# REFERENCES

A simple plan. (2000, February). *Z Magazine, 13*(2), 6–7.

Adamson, N., Briskin, L., & McPhail, M. (1988). *Feminist organizing for change: The contemporary women's movement in Canada.* Toronto, ON: Oxford University Press.

Albert, M., Cagan, L., Chomsky, N., Hahnel, R., King, M., Sargent, L., & Sklar, H. (1986). *Liberating theory.* Cambridge, MA: South End Press.

Alinsky, S.D. (1971). *Rules for radicals: A pragmatic primer for realistic radicals.* New York, NY: Vintage Books.

Arnopoulos, S. (1970, July 16). Two days without sleep: Welfare protesters still have no answer. *The Montreal Daily Star,* p. 21.

Atlas, J. (2010). *Seeds of change: The story of America's most controversial antipoverty community organizing group.* Nashville, TN: Vanderbilt University Press.

Barker, J. (1999). *Street level democracy: Political settings at the margins of global power.* Toronto, ON: Between the Lines.

Bayat, A. (2010). *Life as politics: How ordinary people change the Middle East.* Palo Alto, CA: Stanford University Press. http://dx.doi.org/10.5117/9789053569115

Benello, G. (1972). Social animation among anglophone groups in Québec. In F. Lesemann & M. Thienot (Eds.), *Animations sociales au Québec* (pp. 435–94). Montreal, QC: École de Service Social, Université de Montréal.

Bond, P. (2008). Reformist reforms, non-reformist reforms and global justice: Activist, NGO and intellectual challenges in the world social forum. *Societies Without Borders, 3,* 4–19. www.brill.nl/swb

Breines, W. (1989). *Community and organization in the New Left, 1962–1968: The great refusal.* New Brunswick, NJ: Rutgers University Press.

Breton, E., Jeppesen, S., Kruzynski, A., & Sarrasin R. (Research Group on Collective Autonomy) (2012). Prefigurative self-governance and self-organization: The influence of antiauthoritarian (pro) feminist, radical queer, and antiracist networks in Quebec. In A. Choudry, J. Hanley, & E. Shragge (Eds.), *Organize! Building from the local for global justice* (pp. 156–73). Oakland, CA: PM Press.

Briskin, L. (1991). Feminist practice: A new approach to evaluating feminist strategy. In J.D. Wine & J.L. Ristock (Eds.), *Women and social change: Feminist activism in Canada* (pp. 24–40). Toronto, ON: Lorimer.

Brodhead, D., Goodings, S., & Brodhead, M. (1997). The company of young Canadians. In B. Wharf & M. Clague (Eds.), *Community organizing: Canadian experiences* (pp. 137–48). Toronto, ON: Oxford University Press.

Browne, J., Franco, M., Negrón-Gonzales, J., & Williams. S. (2005). *Towards land, work and power—Charting a path of resistance to US-led imperialism.* San Francisco, CA: Unite to Fight Press.

Browne, P.L. (2001). Rethinking globalization, class and the state. *Canadian Review of Social Policy, 48*(Fall), 93–102.

Bruyn, S.T. (1987). Beyond the market and the state. In S.T. Bruyn & J. Meehan (Eds.), *Beyond the state and the market: New directions in community development* (pp. 3–27). Philadelphia, PA: Temple University Press.

Bruyn, S.T. & Meehan, J. (Eds.). (1987). *Beyond the state and the market: New directions in community development.* Philadelphia, PA: Temple University Press.

Cabaj, M. (Ed.) (2011). *Cities reducing poverty—How Vibrant Communities are creating comprehensive solutions to the most complex problem of our times* (p. 47–64). Waterloo, ON: Tamarack Institute.

Callahan, M. (1997). Feminist community organizing in Canada: Postcards from the edge. In B. Wharf & M. Clague (Eds.), *Community organizing: Canadian experiences* (pp. 181–204). Toronto, ON: Oxford University Press.

Cervero, R., & Wilson, A. (2001). At the heart of practice: The struggle for knowledge and power. In R. Cervero, A. Wilson, et al. (Eds.), *Power in practice: Adult education for knowledge and power in society* (pp. 1–21). San Francisco, CA: Jossey-Bass.

Chaskin, R.J., Joseph, M.L., & Chipenda-Dansokho, S. (1998). Implementing comprehensive community development: Possibilities and limitations. In P. Ewalt, E. Freeman, & D. Poole (Eds.), *Community building: Renewal, well-being and shared responsibility* (pp. 17–28). Washington, DC: NASW Press. http://dx.doi.org/10.1093/sw/42.5.435

Chic Resto-Pop. (1995). *Déclaration des travailleurs et travailleuses exclus.* Montreal: n.p.

Choudry, A., Hanley, J., Jordan, S., Shragge, E., & Stiegman, M. (2009). *Fight back: Workplace justice for immigrants.* Halifax, NS: Fernwood Books.

Church, K. (1997). Business (not quite) as usual: Psychiatric survivors and community economic development in Ontario. In E. Shragge (Ed.), *Community economic development: In search of empowerment* (pp. 48–71). Montreal, QC: Black Rose Books.

Clarke, S.E., & Gaile, G.L. (1998). *The work of cities.* Minneapolis, MN: University of Minnesota Press.

Cloward, R.A., & Piven, F.F. (1977). *Poor people's movements: Why they succeed and how they fail.* New York: Pantheon Books.

Cloward, R.A., & Piven, F.F. (1999). Disruptive dissensus: People and power in the industrial age. In J. Rothman (Ed.), *Reflections on community organization: Enduring themes and critical issues* (pp. 165–93). Itasca, IL: F.E. Peacock.

Collectif des entreprises d'insertion. Retrieved April 26, 2012, from www.collectif.qc.ca.

Cox, Fred M. (1974). *Strategies of community organization: A book of readings.* Itasca, IL: F.E. Peacock.

Crawford, C., Das Gupta, T., Ladd, D., & Vosko, L. (2006). Thinking through community unionism in precarious employment. In L. Vosko (Ed.), *Understanding labour market insecurity in Canada* (pp. 353–77). Montreal/Kingston, ON: McGill-Queen's.

Daly, M. (1970). *The revolution game.* Toronto, ON: New Press.

DeFilippis, J., Fisher, R., & Shragge, E. (2010). *Contesting community—The limits and potential of local organizing.* New Brunswick, NJ: Rutgers University Press.

Delgado, G. (2009) Does ACORN's work contribute to movement building? In R. Fisher (Ed.), *The people shall rule: ACORN, community organizing, and the struggle for economic justice* (pp. 251–74). Nashville, TN: Vanderbilt University Press.

Doucet, L., & Favreau, L. (1991). *Théorie et pratiques en organisation communautaire.* Quebec City, QC: Presses de l'Université du Québec.

Drier, P. (2009) Community organizing: ACORN and progressive politics in America. In R. Fisher (Ed.), *The people shall rule: ACORN, community organizing, and the struggle for economic justice* (pp. 3–39). Nashville, TN: Vanderbilt University Press.

Drover, G., & Shragge, E. (1979). Urban struggle and organizing strategies. *Our Generation, 13*(1), 61–76.

Evans, S., & Boyte, H. (1992). *Free spaces: The sources of democratic change in America* (2nd ed.). Chicago, IL: University of Chicago Press.

Ewalt, P. (1998). The revitalization of impoverished communities. In P. Ewalt, E. Freeman, & D. Poole (Eds.), *Community building: Renewal, well-being and shared responsibility* (pp. 3–5). Washington, DC: NASW Press.

Ewalt, P., Freeman, E., & Poole, D. (Eds.). (1998). *Community building: Renewal, well-being and shared responsibility.* Washington, DC: NASW Press.

Favreau, L. (1989). *Mouvement populaire et intervention communautaire de 1960 à nos jours, continuités et ruptures.* Montreal, QC: Centre de formation populaire et Éditions du fleuve.

Ferrante, A. (1972, February 8). Family allowance proposal: Welfare hikes held up until accord "a reality." *The Montreal Daily Star,* p. 3.

Fine, J. (2006). *Workers centers: Organizing communities at the edge of the dream.* Ithaca, NY: Cornell University Press.

Fisher, R. (1994). *Let the people decide: Neighborhood organizing in America* (rev. ed.). New York, NY: Twayne Publishers.

Fisher, R. (1999). The importance of history and context in community organization. In J. Rothman (Ed.), *Reflections on community organization: Enduring themes and critical issues* (pp. 335–53). Itasca, IL: F.E. Peacock.

Fisher, R., Brooks, F., & Russell, D. (2009). "Don't be a blockhead." ACORN, protest tactics and organizational scale. In R. Fisher (Ed.), *The people shall rule: ACORN, community organizing, and the struggle for economic justice* (pp. 206–34). Nashville, TN: Vanderbilt University Press.

Fisher, R., & Shragge, E. (2000). Challenging community organizing: Facing the 21st century. *Journal of Community Practice, 8*(3), 1–19. http://dx.doi.org/10.1300/J125v08n03_01

Foley, G. (1999). *Learning in social action: A contribution to understanding informal education.* London and New York, NY: Zed Books.

Fontan, J.-M. (1988). Développement économique communautaire à Montréal. *Possibles 12*(2), 12–23.

Fontan, J.-M. (1993). *A critical review of Canadian, American, and European Community economic development literature*. Vancouver, BC: CCE/Westcoast Publications.

Fontan, J.-M. (1994). Le développement économique communautaire québécois: Éléments de synthèse et point de vue critique. *Lien social et politiques—RIAC, 32*, 115–26.

Fontan, J.-M., Hamel, P., Morin, R., & Shragge, E. (2006). Urban perspectives on CED practice: The Montreal experience. In E. Shragge & M. Toye (Eds.), *Community economic development: Building for social change* (pp. 108–24). Sydney, NS: Cape Breton University Press.

Fontan, J.-M., & Shragge, E. (1996). Chic Resto-Pop: New community practice in Quebec. *Community Development Journal: An International Forum, 31*(4), 291–301.

Fontan, J.-M., & Shragge, E. (1998). Community economic development organizations in Montreal. *Journal of Community Practice, 5*(1–2), 125–36. http://dx.doi.org/10.1300/J125v05n01_08

Frank, F., & Smith, A. (1999). *The community development handbook: A tool to build community capacity*. Ottawa, ON: Human Resources Development Canada.

Gindin, S. (2002). Social justice and globalization. *Monthly Review (New York, N.Y.), 54*(2), 1–11.

Goldberg, H. (2008) Building power in the city: Reflections on the emergence of the Right to the City Alliance and the National Domestic Worker's Alliance. Retrieved July 12, 2012, from www.inthemiddleofthewhirlwind.wordpress.com.

Goldberg, H. (2010) Building power in the city: Reflections on the emergence of the Right to the City Alliance and the National Domestic Workers Alliance. In Team Colors Collective (Eds.), *Uses of a Whirlwind: Movement, Movements and Contemporary Radical Currents in the United States* (pp. 97–108). Edinburgh: AK Press.

Gordon, J. (2005). *Suburban sweatshops—The fight for immigrant rights*. Cambridge, MA: The Belknap Press of Harvard University Press.

GMAPCC. (1972). *Statement of principles for the Greater Montreal Anti-Poverty Coordinating Committee*. Montreal, QC: Greater Montreal Anti-Poverty Coordinating Committee.

Gutierrez, L.M., & Lewis, E. (1995). A feminist perspective on organizing with women of color. In F.G. Rivera & J.L. Erlich (Eds.), *Community organizing in a diverse society* (2nd ed) (pp. 95–112). Boston, MA: Allyn and Bacon.

Hamel, P., & Léonard, J.-F. (1980). Ambivalence des luttes urbaines et ambiguïté des interventions de l'état. *Revue Internationale d'Action Communautaire, 4*(44), 74–82.

Hasson, S., & Ley, D. (1994). *Neighbourhood organizations and the welfare state*. Toronto, ON: University of Toronto Press.

Hayden, T. (1988). *Reunion: A memoir*. New York, NY: Collier Books.

Homan, M. (1999). *Promoting community change: Making it happen in the real world* (2nd ed.). Pacific Grove, CA: Brooks Cole Publishing Company.

Hugill, H., & Brogan, P. (2011) The everyday violence of urban neoliberalism: An interview with Nik Theodore. *MRZine*. Retrieved May 15, 2012, from http://mrzine.monthlyreview.org/2011/theodore050411.html.

INCITE! Women of color against violence (Eds.). (2007). *The revolution will not be funded: Beyond the non-profit industrial complex*. Boston, MA: South End Press.

Kamat, S. (2004). The privatization of public interest: Theorizing NGO discourse in a neoliberal era. *Review of International Political Economy*, *11*(1), 155–76. http://dx.doi.org/10.1080/0969229042000179794

Kanuga, M., and Bluestockings Bookstore and Activist Center. (2010). Bluestockings Bookstore and new institutions of self-organized work: The space between common notions and common institutions. In Team Colors Collective (Eds.), *Uses of a Whirlwind—Movement, Movements, and Contemporary Radical Currents in the United States* (pp. 19–36). Oakland, CA: AK Press.

Keck, J., & Fulks, W. (1997). Meaningful work and community betterment: The case of Opportunities for Youth and Local Initiatives Program (1971–1973). In B. Wharf & M. Clague (Eds.), *Community organizing: Canadian experiences* (pp. 113–36). Toronto, ON: Oxford University Press.

Kelly, K., & Caputo, T. (2011). *Community—A contemporary analysis of policies, programs and practices*. Toronto: University of Toronto Press.

Kovel, J. (2002). *The enemy of nature: The end of capitalism or the end of the world?* Halifax, NS: Fernwood Press.

Kretzmann, J., & McKnight, J. (1993). *Building communities from the inside out: A path toward finding and mobilizing a community's assets*. Chicago, IL: Acta Publications.

Kruzynski, A., & Shragge, E. (1999). Getting organized: Antipoverty organizing and social citizenship in the 1970s. *Community Development Journal: An International Forum*, *34*(4), 328–39.

Lavoie, J., Panet-Raymond, J., et al. (2011). *La pratique de l'action communautaire* (3rd ed.). Quebec City, QC: Presses de l'Université du Québec.

Laxer, J. (1996). *In search of a New Left: Canadian politics after the neoconservative assault*. Toronto, ON: Viking Press.

Lemert, C. (1993). *Social theory: The multicultural and classic readings*. Boulder, CO: Westview Press.

Lotz, J. (1997). The beginning of community development in English-speaking Canada. In B. Wharf & M. Clague (Eds.), *Community organizing: Canadian experiences* (pp. 15–28). Toronto, ON: Oxford University Press.

Lotz, J. (1998). *The lichen factor: The quest for community development in Canada*. Sydney, NS: University College of Cape Breton Press.

Loxley, J., Silver, J., & Sexsmith, K. (Eds.). (2007). *Doing community economic development*. Halifax, NS: Fernwood Books.

Lustiger-Thaler, H., & Shragge, E. (1993). Social movements and social welfare: The political problem of needs. In G. Drover & P. Kearns (Eds.), *New approaches to welfare theory* (pp. 161–76). Aldershot, UK: Edward Elgar.

Lynch, H. (2005–2006). Industrial Areas Foundation. *New York Law School Law Review*, *50*, 571–78.

Mann, E. (2011). *Playbook for progressives: 16 qualities of the successful organizer*. Boston, MA: Beacon Press.

Marcuse, P. (2009). From critical urban theory to the right to the city. *City*, *13*(2–3), 185–97. http://dx.doi.org/10.1080/13604810902982177

Marcuse P. (2012, March 25). Reforms, radical reforms and transformative claims [blog post]. Retrieved July 25, 2012, from http://pmarcuse.wordpress.com/2012/03/25/11-blog-11-reforms-radical-reformstransformative-claims/.

Mayer, M. (2009). The 'Right to the City' in the context of shifting mottos of urban social movements. *City*, *13*(2–3), 362–74. http://dx.doi.org/10.1080/13604810902982755

McGrath, S., Moffat, K., & George, U. (1999). Community capacity: The emperor's new clothes. *Canadian Review of Social Policy, 44*, 9–23.

McKnight, J. (1995). *The careless society: Community and its counterfeits.* New York, NY: Basic Books.

McKnight, J., & Block, P. (2010). *The abundant community—Awakening the power of families and neighborhoods.* San Francisco, CA: Berett-Koehler Publishers.

Miller, J. (1987). *Democracy in the streets: From Port Huron to the siege of Chicago.* New York, NY: Simon and Schuster.

Minkler, M., & Wallerstein, N. (1999). Improving health through community organization and community building: A health education perspective. In M. Minkler (Ed.), *Community organizing and community building for health* (pp. 30–52). New Brunswick, NJ: Rutgers University Press.

Morris, D. (1996). Communities: Building authority, responsibility, and capacity. In J. Mander & E. Goldsmith (Eds.), *The case against the global economy and for a turn toward the local* (pp. 434–45). San Francisco, CA: Sierra Club.

Morrison, R. (1995). *Ecological democracy.* Boston, MA: South End Press.

Naparstek, A.J., & Dooley, D. (1998). Countering urban disinvestment through community-building initiatives. In P. Ewalt, E. Freeman, & D. Poole (Eds.), *Community building: Renewal, well being and shared responsibility* (pp. 6–16). Washington, DC: NASW Press.

Ninacs, W. (1997). Entraide économique, création d'entrprises, politiques sociales et "empowerment." *Nouvelles Pratiques Sociales, 8*(1), 97–119. http://dx.doi.org/10.7202/301307ar

Our Generation. (1969). Editorial: Towards an extra-parliamentary opposition in Canada. *Our Generation, 6*(4), 3–19.

Panet-Raymond, J. (1987). Community groups in Québec: From radical action to voluntarism for the state. *Community Development Journal, 22*(4), 281–86. http://dx.doi.org/10.1093/cdj/22.4.281

Panet-Raymond, J. (1992). Partnership: Myth or reality? *Community Development Journal, 27*, 156–65.

Panet-Raymond, J., & Mayer, R. (1997). The history of community development in Quebec. In B. Wharf & M. Clague (Eds.), *Community organizing: Canadian experiences* (pp. 29–61). Toronto, ON: Oxford University Press.

Peck, J., & Tickell, A. (2002). Neoliberalizing space. In N. Brenner & N. Theodore (Eds.), *Spaces of neoliberalization: Urban restructuring in North America and Western Europe* (pp. 33–57). Oxford: Blackwell.

Perera, G. (2008). Claiming the right to the city: A question on power. *Race, Poverty & the Environment, 15*(1), 12–13. Retrieved May 12, 2012, from http://www.urbanhabitat.org/files/15.Perera.pdf

PERM (Pointe St. Charles Equal Rights Movement). (1971). Videotape. Montreal: Parallel Institute.

Popple, K. (1995). *Analysing community work: Its theory and practice.* Bristol, UK: Open University Press.

Popple, K., & Redmond, M. (2000). Community development and the voluntary sector in the new millennium: The implications of the Third Way in the UK. *Community Development Journal, 35*(4), 391–400. http://dx.doi.org/10.1093/cdj/35.4.391

Putnam, R.D. (1995). "Bowling alone": America's declining social capital. *Journal of Democracy, 6*(1), 65–78. http://dx.doi.org/10.1353/jod.1995.0002

Radwanski, G. (1970, July 7). Polite sit-in: Anti-poverty group wins at city hall. *The Montreal Gazette,* p. 73.

Rathke, W. (2009). *Citizen wealth—Winning the campaign to save working families*. San Francisco: Berrett-Koehler Publishers.

Renaud P. (2008). Rapport de l'évaluation du Chantier de revitalisation sociale et urbaine du quartier Saint-Michel à Montréal de 2004 à 2008. Retrieved May 25, 2012, from http://www.vsmsante.qc.ca/uploads/pdf/Evaluation-VSMS.pdf.

Restaurant Opportunity Center. Retrieved July 26, 2012, from www.rocny.org.

Right to the City Alliance—National Organization. (2011). 21st century cities—A strategy to win. Retrieved November 25, 2012, from http://righttothecity.org/downloads/21st-Century-Cities.pdf.

Ristock, J.L. (1991). Feminist collectives: The struggles in our quest for a "uniquely feminist structure." In J.D. Wine & J.L. Ristock (Eds.), *Women and social change: Feminist activism in Canada* (pp. 41–55). Toronto, ON: Lorimer.

Roseland, M. (1998). *Toward sustainable communities: Resources for citizens and their governments*. Gabriola Island, BC: New Society Publishers.

Rothman, J. (1974). Three models of community organization practice. In F. Cox, J.L. Erlich, J. Rothman, & J. Tropman (Eds.), *Strategies of community organization: A book of readings* (pp. 22–39). Itasca, IL: F.E. Peacock.

Rothman, J. (1999a). A very personal account of the intellectual history of community organization. In J. Rothman (Ed.), *Reflections on community organization: Enduring themes and critical issues* (pp. 215–34). Itasca, IL: F.E. Peacock.

Rothman, J. (1999b). Historical context in community intervention. In J. Rothman (Ed.), *Reflections on community organization: Enduring themes and critical issues* (pp. 27–49). Itasca, IL: F.E. Peacock.

Rubin, H.J., & Rubin, I.S. (1992). *Community organizing and community development* (2nd ed). New York, NY: Macmillan.

Shragge, E. (1990). Community based practice: Political alternatives or new state forms? In L. Davies & E. Shragge (Eds.), *Bureaucracy and community* (pp. 137–73). Montreal, QC: Black Rose Books.

Shragge, E. (1994). Anti-poverty movements: Strategies and approaches. *City Magazine*, 15(2/3), 27–9.

Shragge, E. (Ed.). (1997). *Community economic development: In search of empowerment*. Montreal, QC: Black Rose Books.

Shragge, E., & Deniger, M.-A. (1997). Quebec's workfare programs: Whose interests? In E. Shragge (Ed.), *Workfare: An ideology for a new underclass* (pp. 17–34). Toronto, ON: Garamond Press.

Shragge, E. & Fontan, J.-M. (Eds.). (2000). *Social economy: International debates and perspectives*. Montreal, QC: Black Rose Books.

Sites, W., Chaskin, R., & Parks, V. (2007). Reframing community practice for the 21st century: Multiple traditions, multiple challenges. *Journal of Urban Affairs*, 29(5), 519–41. http://dx.doi.org/10.1111/j.1467-9906.2007.00363.x

Stout, L. (1996). *Bridging the class divide and other lessons for grassroots organizing*. Boston, MA: Beacon Press.

Stoecker, R. (2001). Community development and community organizing: Apples and oranges? Chicken and egg? Retrieved May 25, 2012, from http://comm-org.wisc.edu/drafts/orgdevppr2c.htm.

Sturgeon, N. (1995). Theorizing movements: Direct action and direct theory. In M. Darnovsky, B. Epstein, & R. Flacks (Eds.), *Cultural politics and social movements* (pp. 35–51). Philadelphia, PA: Temple University Press.

Swack, M. (1992). *Community economic development: An alternative to traditional development*. Manchester, NH: Mimeo.

Swift, J. (1999). *Civil society in question*. Toronto, ON: Between the Lines.

Teodori, M. (Ed.). (1969). *The New Left: A documentary history*. New York, NY: Bobbs-Merrill.

Terkel, S. (2005). Community in action [radio program]. Retrieved August 28, 2012, from http://www.npr.org/templates/story/story.php?storyId=4963443.

Torjman, S. (1997). *Civil society: Reclaiming our humanity*. Ottawa, ON: Caledon Institute of Social Policy.

Toye, M. (2011). Building momentum for change in Montreal. In M. Cabaj (Ed.), *Cities reducing poverty—How Vibrant Communities are creating comprehensive solutions to the most complex problem of our times* (p. 47–64). Waterloo, ON: Tamarack Institute.

Toye, M., & Charland, N. (2006). CED in Canada: A review of definitions and profiles of practice. In E. Shragge & M. Toye (Eds.), *Community economic development: Building for social change* (pp. 9–20). Sydney, NS: Cape Breton University Press.

United Nations Secretary General. (1955). *Social progress through community development*. New York, NY: United Nations Bureau of Social Affairs.

Veltmeyer, H. (2007). *Illusions and opportunities: Civil society in the quest for social change*. Halifax, NS: Fernwood.

Warren, M.R. (2001). *Dry bones rattling: Community building to revitalize American democracy*. Princeton, NJ: Princeton University Press.

Wharf, B., & Clague, M. (Eds.). (1997). *Community organizing: Canadian experiences*. Toronto, ON: Oxford University Press.

White, D. (1997). Contradictory participation: Reflections on community action in Quebec. In B. Wharf & M. Clague (Eds.), *Community organizing: Canadian experiences* (pp. 62–90). Toronto, ON: Oxford University Press.

Williams, D. (1997). *The road to now—A history of Blacks in Montreal*. Montreal: Véhicule Press.

# INDEX